# Chenrezig
## THE PRACTICE OF COMPASSION

A Commentary by
## Ringu Tulku Rinpoche

11 Crofts Street, London, E1 8LU, UK
www.rigultrust.org  info@rigultrust.org

**Published by Rigul Trust**
**Text ©2011 Ringu Tulku**
Ringu Tulku asserts the moral right to be identified as the author of this work.
Please do not reproduce any part of this book without permission from the publisher.

Second Edition. October 2022.
ISBN  978-0-9957343-8-8

This Chenrezig commentary originated as an oral teaching given by Ringu Tulku Rinpoche in Halscheid, Germany, in November 1998.

Transcribed and edited by Corinne Segers with further editing by Caitlin Collins.
Chenrezig painting and drawing by R. D. Salga.
Typesetting and design by Paul O'Connor at Judo Design, Ireland.
Photographs of Rigul, Kham, Tibet by Francois Henrard.

The root text used here was originally translated by Tyler Dewar of the Nitartha Translation Network, under the guidance of Dzogchen Ponlop Rinpoche, with reference to a previous translation by the Nālandā Translation Committee. Originally published in 'Trainings in Compassion: Manuals on the Meditation of Avalokiteshvara' *(Ithaca: Snow Lion Publications, 2004)* It has been re-printed here with the generous permission of Snow Lion Publications.

*I am the jewel in the lotus*

# CONTENTS

| | |
|---|---:|
| INTRODUCTION | 1 |
| THE COMMENTARY | 7 |
| Refuge | 8 |
| Bodhichitta | 14 |
| Visualisation of Chenrezig | 17 |
| Praise | 26 |
| The Seven Branch Prayer | 27 |
| Prayer for Liberating Beings from the Six Realms | 33 |
| Self-Visualisation as Chenrezig | 39 |
| Mantra Recitation | 43 |
| Pure appearances | 54 |
| The Dissolution | 61 |

|     |     |
| --- | --- |
| Re-emergence and Dedication | 62 |
| Additional Prayers and Phowa | 64 |
| Conclusion: The Devotional Approach | 67 |

## Discussion   73

|     |     |
| --- | --- |
| Dedication | 101 |

## All-Pervading Benefit of Beings   103

The Meditation and Recitation of the Great Compassionate One

## Glossary   139

## Acknowledgements   144

## Commemorating Ringu Tulku Rinpoche's Homeland in Tibet   147

# INTRODUCTION

The Chenrezig sadhana that I will explain to you is a very simple practice. It's the shortest and most popular text of the sadhana that was composed by Thangtong Gyalpo. Thangtong Gyalpo (1385-1464) was a well known and very great master in Tibet. It's difficult to categorise him into any particular lineage or tradition but, although he stood alone, he is a totally uncontroversial figure. Absolutely everybody from all the different schools acknowledges his greatness.

Some people say that he lived at least 150 years, others that he lived more than 500 years. He was active in various fields, like social work for instance. He built many iron bridges, I think thirteen or fourteen, in Tibet and Bhutan, some of which are still used. They were big iron bridges, made with thick iron chains, twisted together into bigger chains, twisted again into bigger chains and then assembled into bridges. He is also the founder of the Tibetan Opera. He wouldn't stay in one place but travelled all over Tibet. Many monasteries are also supposed to have been founded by him, among them the great Dergay Monastery, with its famous press, the biggest Tibetan xylograph press (he started the monastery, not the press). He was a very great being and this particular sadhana, although quite short and simple, is therefore regarded as particularly powerful and charged with great blessings.

Chenrezig – or Avalokiteshvara in Sanskrit – is the name of the bodhisattva who is regarded as the Lord of Compassion or the embodiment of compassion. The bodhisattva of compassion can be considered in two ways. From a historical or mundane point of view we can say that Avalokiteshvara was a person like us, living a very long time ago, who felt infinite compassion towards all sentient beings and who was so tremendously courageous that he committed himself to postpone his own enlightenment until he had brought all other beings to that state of perfect liberation. He is the greatest example of complete courage and unselfish compassion. Another approach is to see him not as a human being, but as compassion embodied in the form of a deity. Avalokiteshvara is a symbolic figure representing the compassion of all sentient beings, of all the Buddhas and bodhisattvas. Not only does this form represent compassion, it completely embodies it.

Chenrezig practice is done in order to develop our own compassion. From the Buddhist point of view, we can try to generate compassion through changing or re-thinking our attitude and working on our way of perceiving things. Then there's another way, which is the one I will mainly explain here, and that is through feeling; it's an experiential, emotional approach.

I think it's important to understand, that, in order to be able to feel compassion and have kind, positive feelings towards others, we first need to know what such feelings are - this requires that we should have experienced receiving them ourselves.

That's precisely one of the main things we work on through the 'deity yoga' which is the core of a sadhana.

For instance, in this practice, we imagine the presence of Chenrezig, the bodhisattva of compassion, on top of our head or in front of us. Whatever we think or say, we have a certain experience linked to the concepts involved; we naturally project something. For example, if you read the name of a place and a description of it, an image of it forms in your mind. In the same way, when we think of the bodhisattva Chenrezig, when we say 'the Lord of Compassion', our concept naturally creates the image of a compassionate being and not of someone who is angry, arrogant or unhappy. When we think about a 'Buddha', an enlightened being, it evokes an image of complete perfection, of somebody without any fault or confusion, who has done away with ignorance, who is totally wise and completely compassionate, who only wants to help and work for the welfare of other beings with no other intention, no selfish motivation.

This is what we visualise or think of in this practice. We feel the presence of Chenrezig, the most courageous bodhisattva who took the commitment not to become enlightened himself until all sentient beings are completely liberated and enlightened. His compassion is of the strongest kind, the kind that inspires one to exchange one's own well being and happiness for the well-being and happiness of others, to always consider others' interests before one's own.

So we think of Chenrezig, who embodies that kind of compassion, who has the will, the wisdom and the capacity to help. It may help for example to think of a person in your life, a true friend, somebody who loves you unconditionally, who always tries to help you without expecting anything in return, and who has the wisdom and the skill to do this in the best possible way. We try to imagine somebody of that nature, who is the very embodiment of compassion. We see Chenrezig as the very essence of the compassion of all the enlightened beings, radiating loving kindness and wisdom.

'Visualising' doesn't mean trying to look at something or to see it as if you were looking at a picture. Of course, if you can visualise as clearly as if you were looking at a picture, that's very good, however visualising is not as if you were sitting there just passively watching a movie. It's more important to get involved in the process, to feel that Chenrezig is actually there, is really present in whatever form you want to visualise him. It doesn't really matter whether you visualise his form in one way or another, although it happens sometimes that a person has a certain connection with a specific form of a particular bodhisattva or Buddha. The form of Chenrezig doesn't really matter because, in a way, it's our own true loving kindness, the root of our basic capacity to love and be compassionate that we project and that is radiating towards us.

We try to feel that we – and all the other beings in the whole universe – receive this loving kindness. We're all basking in the light and warmth of the loving kindness radiating from this being who is the embodiment of all the enlightened beings. Without conceptualising this too much, we try to physically feel the radiance of loving kindness and the well-being of receiving it. We feel that our inner heart is being penetrated by this radiance and that we are really opening up to it. We feel that we, and all the other beings, are always in the presence and under the protection of this enlightened being who is continuously radiating his help and unconditional loving kindness towards us.

Although we don't need to conceptualise this too much, there are two aspects in the meditation I've just described. One aspect is that we are generating and developing loving kindness in ourselves by receiving it, by feeling it, while the other is that we are letting our mind relax, because we naturally relax when we feel loving kindness. So it's simultaneously a meditation that makes our mind calm and peaceful, and a process of generating loving kindness.

# The Commentary

Any Buddhist practice starts with taking refuge and, if it is a Mahayana practice, refuge is accompanied by the development of bodhichitta. This is what we find in the beginning of the sadhana:

*Sang gye chö dang tshok kyi chok nam la*
*Chang chub bar du dak ni kyap su chi*
*Dak gi jin sok gyi pe sö nam kyi*
*Dro la phen chir sang gye drup par shok*

It means, through all the positive deeds, like giving, etc, and all the positive results coming from that, may I attain enlightenment for the benefit of all sentient beings.

The first two lines are the refuge and the next two the development of bodhichitta. I don't think it is necessary for me to explain in detail the meaning of refuge and bodhichitta this time but, as it's a very important subject, I'll say a few words about it.

# Refuge

Refuge is not only the formal ceremony that marks somebody's entrance into Buddhism; nor is it just a preliminary to Buddhist practice. Taking refuge encompasses the entire Buddhist practice: it sets our goal or purpose and defines the path to follow as well as the way to travel on it. It is therefore essential: we could say in a way that there's actually nothing else in Buddhism but taking refuge. All the Buddhist teachings and practices are contained within it because everything is included in the Buddha, the Dharma and the Sangha.

We can consider it from different angles, talk about it at different levels, place the emphasis on different aspects, but the main point remains the fundamental desire of every being – not only human beings but actually every sentient being – to be happy, to have what is pleasurable, and to be free from suffering, problems and pain. All beings wish for everlasting happiness and that is where everything starts. All of us are busy running around, worried and anxious, because of this basic desire for happiness. But however much we pursue happiness still we are not happy, because we don't really understand how to find the happiness we seek. And when we look a little deeper into our predicament, we may wonder whether it is possible to realise this fundamental aspiration. How can we achieve it?

Our usual way is to look for certain things, certain situations that we believe will make us happy. We try different ways and means to get such things and situations only to find out afterwards that they are not real sources of happiness. Indeed, they are impermanent, and can even themselves become the cause of further problems. They are not lasting solutions to our problems; they are not real sources of happiness.

If we then reconsider the situation and try to find out what is really making us happy or unhappy, we are led back to our own mind. Happiness and unhappiness do not come from the things and situations we create but from the way our mind reacts, the way our mind functions.

When I use the word 'mind' here, I do not only mean the thinking mind, but also perceptions, emotions, feelings, sensations – the whole of our experience.

If we could find a way to work on the mind and change our usual way of reacting, might it be possible to find a state of mind that doesn't bring us pain, suffering and problems? This would mean working less on the things and situations that we experience, and more on the 'experiencer', of these things. From the Buddhist point of view, to be able to change one's way of experiencing in a particular context and situation is the main objective. Therefore the main Buddhist practice comes down to working on our mind – that is on our own experience.

How things appear for me depends on the way I experience them. Two people placed in the same situation may experience it and therefore react to it in two very different ways. The way we experience something is the most important factor because that is where all our happiness and unhappiness come from. In a given situation, I may react in such a way that everything is fine and no problem for me, or I may also react differently and feel very unhappy. It all depends on the way I react.

This is why, in the Buddhist approach, we are essentially working on the way we react. In order to do this, we have to talk about our emotions and perceptions. If we can transform all our negative emotions and impure perceptions, nothing else is needed because we will then be completely happy and peaceful. That is Buddhahood. Buddha, or Buddhahood, is nothing but a state in which the mind constantly remains positive and never reacts with negative emotions, never gets overpowered by them. That state of mind is completely free from problems, which is why it is called enlightenment or Buddhahood.

This can only come about when one has a real and deep understanding, a deep realisation, of how to work with the mind. It means that one can see oneself very clearly, without illusions, delusions, obstacles, hindrances or confusion of any kind. With that understanding and experience, one can transform emotions. That is sometimes regarded as the highest form of Dharma. It is also sometimes called the Buddha, because this absolute, perfect Dharma is nothing but the absolute, perfect state of Buddhahood. The realisation of Dharma is the Buddha; so it doesn't really make much difference whether you call it Buddha or Dharma. The Dharma comprises all the various ways, paths, means, methods and techniques used in order to realise the state of Buddha.

The people who tread these paths, who practise the Dharma in a genuine way, are the Sangha. However, the ultimate or highest form of Sangha is also the Buddha. It is therefore sometimes said that the true absolute refuge is only the Buddha and that the two other aspects of Dharma and Sangha are included in the Buddha.

Although in the beginning the Buddha, Dharma and Sangha are presented as three separate refuges, they really refer to this true realisation, this complete transformation of our usual way of reacting, which, as long as it is confused, unclear and based on a misunderstanding, is the source of our sufferings, problems and unhappiness.

Our usual, mistaken way of reacting is called samsara. As long as we react in this way, we can never be completely happy because, at the most basic level, our reactions are wrong: they are not in accord with reality.

We could identify the pattern as follows. We want something; then we make great efforts to try to get it. That very struggle to get happiness brings worries and anxiety. You see, this way of going about it is wrong right from the beginning. It's as if we come to sit near a fire in order to get cool. The cooler we want to be, the closer to the fire we sit! It isn't going to work, and this is more or less what we're doing all the time.

It reminds me of the story of a Tibetan man who went on pilgrimage to Bodhgaya and came back complaining that India was so terribly hot that even when he heaped nine blankets around his body, the heat still wouldn't go away. In Tibet, heat is not a problem: the only problem is cold. If the cold is very intense, you cover yourself with more blankets and, usually, under nine blankets, you no longer feel the cold. So he thought he could fend off the heat in the same way as he'd protected himself from the cold.

We need to change our habitual way of reacting through the practice. However, we should be careful not to practise the Dharma in the way we usually do everything else, otherwise there will be no difference! If we practise Dharma in order to get things, we'll just become more samsaric, because we're practising even the Dharma in a samsaric way.

What matters is not so much what we do, but how we do it. That's why meditation is so important. Through meditation, we try to make our mind calmer, more relaxed, more spacious, more peaceful, to release the anxiety, the worries, the struggle. If our meditation is tight and nervous, full of anxieties, and if we 'struggle' to meditate, we will never achieve anything. We need to learn how to work on our mind: that's the Dharma practice.

It's all very well to say that we have to practise Dharma – but the question is - How? We try to visualise and to meditate, but what does meditation really mean? If we don't clarify this question, we'll fall into the trap of a mistaken, samsaric practice. We may call it Dharma but it's actually no different from samsara – which is why Gampopa repeated this warning again and again: "If you don't practise Dharma as Dharma, the Dharma will lead you to the lower realms!" So to practise Dharma means to work on our mind, on the way we react.

'Taking refuge in the Buddha, the Dharma and the Sangha is the first thing we do in our practice. By taking refuge we set our goal, our intention. Without an objective, we're lost, confused, we don't know what to do or what is important and what is not. A lack of purpose in life is a big problem that places us in a very difficult position. First we get bored and then, after some time, we feel confused and useless, we are incapable of doing anything useful. Then, because we don't have a purpose, we feel worthless and fall into depression.

I think it's very important to find a purpose. I sincerely believe that one can never become depressed if one has a really good objective in life. When people have a sense of purpose, they may go through incredible suffering and hardship without psychological problems, while those who lead an aimless life are more likely to have such problems. Taking refuge means asserting a great and beneficial purpose.

First, we take refuge in the Buddha. Of course, to understand the Buddha is not easy; it encompasses the whole practice and experience of Buddhism. However, we should at least have this concept that Buddha is the complete realisation, the complete eradication of all confusion and ignorance, a state of being that corresponds to the transformation of all the negative emotions. We should know that this is the true state of our mind. And that is what we want to realise, to actualise, what we ourselves would like to be. We would like to de-condition ourselves from our confused state of mind and return to the true primordial state of our mind, which is the Buddha nature. That is our purpose. That is our objective. And we don't want it just for ourselves but for all other sentient beings as well. They all suffer and they all want to attain everlasting peace and happiness, and it is for them also that we want to become enlightened. We wish to bring them all to that state of enlightenment. That commitment is going for refuge to the Buddha. It generally consists of two aspects: the wish to do it and the conviction that it is possible. It is not easy even to simply understand it, but that is the main thing.

In order to achieve our goal, we take refuge in the Dharma. The Dharma encompasses all the different means, practices and trainings that would lead us to that realisation or actualisation. Taking refuge in the Dharma is the expression of our wish to train in those practices.

Finally, taking refuge in the Sangha is our readiness to open ourselves to those who have the understanding and experience of the teachings and methods, in order to learn these ways and means. We open ourselves to receive the positive influence, the instructions and teachings of the Dharma so that we can work on ourselves.

The whole of Buddhism is included in these three facets of the refuge. Having taken refuge, we know what we want and what we need to do, so we work on that and create the right circumstances that will enable us to do it. The refuge is therefore the entire Buddhist practice. There's actually nothing more in Buddhism than taking refuge.

It may seem easy to understand at an intellectual level but a full understanding is more difficult than we first imagine. Even the possibility of enlightenment and its implications aren't easy to fathom. A real, deep desire to achieve it is difficult to develop because we are too influenced and so overpowered by our emotions that our desire is not usually oriented towards that end.

Nevertheless, even if it's not easy, it's the most important thing. Of course everybody wants happiness, but the question is what will bring us real happiness, real peace? We need to remind ourselves of our commitment to work in that direction and to revive our inspiration and understanding, again and again. This is why we repeat the refuge prayer daily and at the beginning of every practice.

I think you now understand the importance of the refuge. I won't go into more details.

# Bodhichitta

There's very little difference between bodhichitta and refuge in the Mahayana approach. The Mahayana refuge is an aspiration or commitment to attain enlightenment for the sake of all sentient beings, which is the same as bodhichitta. The main point here is to develop the thought: 'I take refuge in Buddha, Dharma and Sangha, and my purpose for doing that is to benefit all sentient beings - not just myself. For the sake of them all, I would like to become a Buddha'.

Bodhichitta is inspired by compassion, limitless compassion. We could define compassion in a general way as unbiased, universal goodwill. It is love but – unlike ordinary love – this is unconditional love. Usually, when we love someone, we expect this person to love us too and if this is not the case, we feel bad. That's conditional love. What we're talking about here is unconditional love. It means that we wish the best for others, whatever they feel towards us. If somebody hates me, it's his or her problem. If somebody loves me, it's also his or her problem. From my side, I have only good wishes, beneficial, positive thoughts and intentions for everybody. I don't worry about the reactions they may have towards me.

From this point of view, being compassionate is not heavy; it's light to bear. From my side, I have no negative feelings towards anybody. I always wish well towards everyone, whether they like me or not, whether they treat me well or not and even whether I like them or not. That is, I think, also important to understand: you don't have to like somebody in order to feel compassion for him or her. Even if you don't like someone, you don't wish him or her bad things. Sometimes people have difficulty developing compassion for someone they dislike because they think that they have to like the person. As they don't, they feel bad and guilty. However, it's not necessary to like somebody in order to feel compassion for him or her. There are people I like and people I don't like. We can't like everybody and that's OK, as long as we just don't wish them bad things.

Having generated compassion, we try to cultivate this motivation or aspiration, to strengthen it and extend its scope. We recognise that it's good for us and good for others. When we don't have any negative thought, any hatred or any ill feeling towards anybody, we already feel peaceful because, in a way, we have forgiven.

Forgiveness means having no ill will or no negative thoughts towards anyone, so we're free from our burden of negative thoughts and hatred. This is beneficial for us, because our mind is clear, free from all the garbage, and we have nothing to hold on to; and, of course, as we no longer hold any negative thoughts against others, it's also good for everybody else.

We become naturally purer and more positive in our being and attitude because there's nobody we consider as an enemy. Everybody is like a friend because we wish everyone well. This doesn't mean that we have to particularly like everybody, but we wish them well and they are therefore like 'unacquainted friends' or 'unknown friends'. This is the attitude we try to generate as we develop our bodhichitta.

The compassion of bodhichitta also includes wishing well to everybody. Moreover, it is boundless or limitless or infinite in four ways.

The first of the four limitless aspects is the wish to see all sentient beings be free from suffering: not just me, my family and my friends: not just the people of my country or those who are Buddhists, or the people of this world; but every single sentient being everywhere throughout the universe.

The second is the wish that they all be free from all suffering, not just a little bit of this or that suffering, but of every kind of suffering.

The third is the wish that they all will not only be free from all suffering but that they also attain the best achievement, the highest form of peace and happiness, which is enlightenment.

The fourth is the wish that they will not only enjoy this highest level of attainment for a short period of time, but forever.

Compassion extended in these four limitless ways becomes bodhichitta. Bodhichitta has two aspects: compassion for all beings, and the commitment to help them attain enlightenment. These two aspects are also called compassion and wisdom. The wisdom aspect is the understanding that a state of everlasting peace and happiness – enlightenment – can be achieved. The compassion aspect is the wish to help all sentient beings to attain that state. These two are like the two wings of a bird: they must always go together.

When we recite this first stanza of the text, we're reminding ourselves of this commitment. We can either imagine that we take refuge and develop the bodhichitta aspiration in front of a Refuge Tree or in the presence of Chenrezig alone, considering him as the embodiment of all the aspects of refuge, of the whole lineage and of our guru. We then take refuge and the bodhichitta commitment to confirm and reiterate our aspiration and understanding. We repeat these four lines three times.

## Visualisation of Chenrezig

Our present purpose is to get in touch with the presence of Chenrezig, an enlightened being who concentrates in himself the energy of all the enlightened beings, of all the Buddhas.

We don't need to engage in conceptual speculations about who or what Chenrezig actually is. What matters is to feel that the real embodiment of unlimited compassion is actually present in the space above us. We imagine all other sentient beings around us, and then either visualise him above our heads or in front of us. It's not just 'my' Chenrezig but everybody's Chenrezig.

The text says:

> *Dak sok kha khyab sem chen gyi*
> *Chi tsuk pe kar da we teng*
> *Hri le phak chok Chen re zi*
> *Kar sal ö zer nga den tro*

This means,

> *On top of the head of myself and all sentient beings,*
> *is a lotus and moon, upon this is a **HRI**.*
> *From the HRI appears the noble Chenrezig,*
> *white in colour, radiating the five colours.*

This starts the process of creating our visualisation of Chenrezig, of creating the form or the way in which he appears.

First we imagine that a very beautiful lotus flower appears one or two feet above our heads. On top of it floats a moon disc on which a letter HRI ( ཧྲཱིཿ ) just drops from nowhere, like a thunderbolt. This letter HRI ( ཧྲཱིཿ ), a very strong white light that spreads in all directions.

This light touches, inspires, and we could almost say 'awakens' all the enlightened beings throughout space. Carrying their blessings, their grace and energy, the light is reabsorbed into the syllable. The light goes out very quickly, and then zooms back into the HRI ( ཧྲཱིཿ ), which is now charged with the blessings and the energies of all the enlightened beings.

Now this very energetic HRI (ཧྲཱིཿ) radiates another set of light rays that touch all sentient beings throughout space. It completely purifies, heals, liberates and transforms all the beings it touches. Having spread throughout space, the light again zooms back into the letter HRI (ཧྲཱིཿ). This HRI (ཧྲཱིཿ) is now even stronger, even more energetic, because not only does it have the energy and the blessings of all the enlightened beings, but also the power of having accomplished the benefit of all the sentient beings.

Thanks to that strong energy and activity, the HRI (ཧྲཱིཿ) transforms into the image of Chenrezig, which is therefore very powerful, very energetic, lively and active. This is what we should try to feel.

Chenrezig is very beautiful. He appears to be young, because compassion is ageless and never decays or deteriorates. His body has what we call the thirty-two major and eighty minor signs of a great being and with all of the beauty and qualities we can imagine belonging to a divine being. He is radiating compassion and wisdom. His colour is white, a colour that represents purity and also compassion. As is described in some texts, he is white like the snowy mountains, when the first rays of the sun shine on their slopes.

We shouldn't categorise Chenrezig as any particular racial type. He's neither Asian nor Western nor African; he's just completely beautiful. He's simply whatever you can imagine as perfection. Maybe the images of the deities are created a little different from usual human beings precisely to avoid their being categorised into one particular racial type; this is not said in any commentary, but it may be a possible explanation.

Chenrezig has four arms, representing the four limitless thoughts, namely love, compassion, rejoicing and equanimity, which means a complete absence of prejudices. His body is not that of a normal human being; it is so full of energy, blessings and activities that it is continuously radiating lights of the five colours.

If it's not too difficult for you to visualise, then you can contemplate the face of this completely kind, radiating being, who has no selfish motive and is only wishing good for everybody else. Or, if you're not very good at visualising, you can just feel his presence, a presence of complete, unconditional kindness, love and compassion.

The description continues:

> *Dze dzum thuk jey chen gyi zik*

This means that he's smiling and looking at all the sentient beings with great kindness, caring for them as if each one were his only child.

And then it goes on:

> *Chak zhi dang po thal jar dze*
> *Ok nyi shel treng pe kar nam*
> *Dar dang rin chen gyen gyi tre*
> *Ri dak pak pe to yok sol*

This is describing how the first two of his four hands are folded together around a wish-fulfilling gem, while he holds a crystal rosary in his other right hand, and a lotus flower in his other left hand. The garments he wears are beautiful, made of the finest colourful silks. He's also wearing a deerskin on his shoulder. This is to symbolise a kind of deer that, like dolphins, always tries to help other beings.

It is believed – I don't know whether this is true or not – that if you're lost in a jungle and you call for help, this animal will come and lead you out of the forest. Many stories are told about this animal; one of them appears in the Jataka tales, the stories relating the Buddha Shakyamuni's former lives.

In this story, a hunter once fell down a cliff and got lost in the jungle. Almost dying, he was crying for help when a beautiful deer appeared and showed him the way out of the forest, thus saving his life. This animal was so extraordinary that the hunter thought the king would reward him for catching it. He told his story to the king and agreed to lead him to the place where he had seen this wonderful animal and help him to catch it, in return for a reward. The king surrounded the forest with his men, who started shooting all the animals they could see.

When the deer heard what was going on, he came face to face with the king and asked him, "Why are you doing this? You should not kill uselessly and senselessly like this. What do you really want?" Hearing the deer speak, the king was very impressed. He explained that he killed animals because he and his subjects had to eat. The deer replied, "It is true you have to eat, but you don't need to kill senselessly as you're doing now. I am the king of the deer. If you agree, we can make an arrangement that will be good for all of us. From now on, I will send a deer to your kitchen every day." Impressed and surprised, the king accepted the deal and returned to his palace.

The next day, a deer appeared at his kitchen door; and the next day, and the next, and every day. But one day, as the king of the deer was walking through the jungle, he heard somebody weeping. Looking around, he saw a doe who was sobbing in despair. When he asked why she was weeping, she answered that it was her turn to go next day to the king's kitchen and that she had just given birth to the small baby lying by her side. Her own death would mean that her baby would surely die too, which was why she was so unhappy. The king of the deer comforted her and told her not to worry, that she wouldn't have to go; the next day, he himself stood near the king's kitchen. He looked so extraordinary that the cooks immediately informed the king that a very special deer had come that day. The king recognised the king of the deer, and asked him:

"Why have you come here yourself? You should have sent one of your subjects."

"Today I have come myself, so you can kill me and eat me."

"This is not right! You are such a wonderful being, and you are the king of the deer. I can't kill you. You must go away at once."

"No. I cannot go because, if I have to send all my people in turn to come to you and be eaten, then when my turn comes, I should also share their fate. If you spare my life because I am the king, how can I deserve my title and lead my people? My turn has come today, so I must take my responsibility."

The king asked him what he could do to spare his life. The deer answered, "You can declare that, from now on, you will no longer require any deer to come here to be killed. You can forbid all the people in your country to hunt deer, and not only the deer but all other animals too. All the animals are like us: they are afraid when they are hunted, tortured and killed. If you give this order, then maybe I will go away."

The king was so surprised and so moved that he agreed immediately and promised to make this announcement that very day. "Now you can go away!" he said.

But the deer was still not satisfied. "The birds in the sky are as badly treated as the other animals by the humans," he said. "So are the fishes in the rivers and lakes. How can I be happy if only the forest animals are saved but the birds and fishes are still being hunted? I don't want to leave if I can only save my people, while the other animals are still not free to live their lives happily."

So the king agreed to issue a royal decree stating that from now on, in his country, nobody would be allowed to hunt or fish or kill any animal, and that every living being would be free. Then the deer thanked the king and went away.

Now the description continues:

*Ö pak me pe u gyen chen*

In the knot of hair on top of Chenrezig's head, there's a small Amitabha. Amitabha is the Buddha of the Padme family. Chenrezig belongs to this 'family' and is regarded as the emanation of Amitabha, which is why this small image is adorning his head.

*Zhap nyi dor je kyil trung zhuk*
*Dri me da war gyap ten pa*
*Kyap ne kun dü ngo wor gyur*

He is sitting in the lotus posture, his back resting on a white moon disc.

It's the presence of this being, the embodiment of the Three Jewels, charged with such deep symbolism and significance, and all the enlightened beings' energies, wisdom and compassion, that we feel and visualise on top of our heads or in front of us.

Although the text doesn't clearly mention anything about the syllables OM MANI PADME HUNG, it is generally understood – although it isn't absolutely necessary – that when we visualise the deity, we also visualise the mantra in his heart.

As I already repeatedly stressed, the main thing in the visualisation is the feeling. We have to really feel the presence, or the energy, or whatever you call it. As in any healing technique, it's our own concentration, our own trust and confidence that draw the blessings, the power, the positive energies of all the enlightened beings.

It has to be clearly understood that, when I mention 'all the enlightened beings', these are not only the Buddhist enlightened beings. From a Buddhist point of view, there is no difference between Buddhist and non-Buddhist enlightened beings. Any being who has reached a high stage of realisation, in whatever way and through whatever tradition, is considered an enlightened being. You can include everybody, all the great beings you know about or haven't yet heard about. You invoke, embodied and concentrated in your visualisation of Chenrezig, the totality of everything that is good, positive, powerful, beneficial, compassionate and wise. That is what you feel!

We don't try too hard to 'concentrate' in this practice. We visualise in the style of a shamatha or shinay meditation, which means that we just let this figure, this image or this presence arise lightly in our mind and we rest in that state. Alternatively, we can also feel the energy, the joyfulness, the goodness, the bliss of the deity, and rest in that feeling. That's also shinay.

If the mind is distracted and wanders around too much, we can sharpen the focus on one particular detail, like Chenrezig's face or eyes, or the letter HRI ( ཧྲཱིཿ ). When the mind is scattered and agitated and we lose control over its movements, that's the moment when we should concentrate on a small object. The smaller the object, the stronger the concentration is. You can visualise the mantra or the syllable HRI ( ཧྲཱིཿ ) in very small but very distinct letters, as if they were written with a single hair. Or if there is mental dullness, it helps to look at something which is hanging and just about to drop or fall down; this makes your mind more alert.

As we are considering this practice from a devotional point of view, it is mainly – as I said in the beginning – the feeling that matters: feeling the warmth, the protection, feeling the trust and comfort of having a friend who has the capacity, the compassion and the wisdom to look after us. This feeling can be nurtured and sustained during our daily life. For instance, when we go to bed, we can feel that we sleep under Chenrezig's protection. From the moment we get up, we can carry on our daily activities in his presence. In this way, we feel protected and strengthened at every moment and we can better face difficulties, anxiety or feelings of fear; this is also an important aspect of the practice. We should understand that this is not something we create artificially, but that these positive qualities are inherent in our very nature, in the Buddha nature that is within us. These qualities are not separate from us, but can also manifest from outside.

# Praise

Having created the visualisation, we then recite this praise:

> *Jo wo kyön gyi ma gö ku dok kar*
> *Dzok sang gye kyi u la gyen*
> *Tuk jey chen gyi dro la zik*
> *Chen re zi la chak tsal lo*

These are the Buddha's own words in praise of Avalokiteshvara, which can be found in both sutras and tantras. This praise is said to have existed even before the Buddha Shakyamuni composed it for us. It is a very simple prayer but it is supposed to be very sacred and to carry many blessings. It can be explained according to several different levels of meaning but, for the moment, we can just stick to the literal meaning of the words.

*'Jo wo'* can approximately be translated as 'Lord'.

*'Kyön gyi ma gö ku dok kar'* means: 'whose white body has never been stained by any defilement'. White is the colour of purity.

*'Dzok sang gye kyi u la gyen'* means: (you have) a perfect Buddha – that is Amitabha – as an ornament above your head.

*'Tuk jey chen gyi dro la zik'*: 'you look with compassionate eyes at all beings.'

*'Chen re zi la chak tsal lo'*: 'to you, Chenrezig, I prostrate.'

We try to develop devotion while reciting this praise as many times as possible and feeling that the lights radiating from Chenrezig's body, carrying his compassion and energy, really penetrate into us. All the other beings around us, throughout space, also receive that energy and are healed by it.

At this point we can add two prayers if we wish. The first is the seven point practice or the Seven Branch Prayer; the second is a prayer for liberating beings from the six realms. These two are added; they are not originally part of this particular short practice. If you only have time for a very brief practice, you can recite one prayer and leave the other or, if you are really too busy, you can skip them both.

# The Seven Branch Prayer

The Seven Branch Prayer is a means of working with seven types of practice on our strongest harmful emotions in order to develop more positive tendencies.

The first branch is *prostration*. Prostration is a way of showing respect; it's a token of submission. When we prostrate we bow down to somebody, acknowledging his or her great qualities. We show humility. Prostrating is working on our pride through developing respect towards others and showing appreciation of their qualities.

Here, we prostrate in a grand way. A bodhisattva's way of doing things is always grand and vast. This means that we don't do it alone but with all other sentient beings alongside us. Not only are we surrounded by all sentient beings all over the universe, we also imagine that countless duplicates of ourselves emanate from our body and that all together we prostrate to Chenrezig and to all the Buddhas of the ten directions and the three times. That means we all prostrate to everybody. The Buddhas of the three times are those of the past and present and also of the future – who are none other than all the sentient beings; we believe that each and every sentient being will one day become a Buddha. The Buddhas of the ten directions are those residing in the east, west, north, and south, in the four directions in-between, and above and below.

The second branch is *making offerings*. Offering means giving, being generous, not holding on or clinging, so this works on our miserliness and the tendency to cling to what we have or desire. Of course, we can offer whatever we want, but the particular offerings mentioned in the text are flowers, incense, lights, music, and objects we find pleasant through the perceptions of our five senses. What we are clinging to, what we are attached to, distracted by, and bound by, are actually the pleasures of our five senses – the beautiful things we see, the fragrances we smell, sweet tastes, soft textures, and the melodious sounds we hear. We now offer whatever we enjoy through our five senses in the form of actual material belongings or offerings created in our imagination.

These practices are basically methods for working on our mind, which is why we offer mental creations as well. Buddhists consider that what really matters is the mental attitude. It doesn't mean, of course, that real offerings are unnecessary or that we shouldn't give real things to other beings. Of course not; the more we give, the better it is. But the point is that here we're working on our mind and, therefore, mental creations do count. Miserliness, clinging and attachment are not necessarily linked to what we actually possess. We don't have to be rich to be very attached to our belongings. One can be very rich and have lots of things without necessarily being too much attached to them. One can also be very rich and completely attached to all one's belongings. But one can also be very poor and desperately cling to whatever worthless things one has. One can even be very much attached to things one doesn't have. What we actually have or don't have is not what determines our degree of attachment. It's rather a way of reacting; it's all in our mind. This is why we're here mainly working on our mind and why we create a mental image of whatever we're attached to, whatever we're grasping at, and then turn it into an offering. It's a mental exercise of letting go.

The third branch is the *purification*, also sometimes called the branch of confession. Offerings and purification are two very important trainings that we also find in the ngondro and almost everywhere in Buddhist practices. They're about being able to let go of the good as well as the bad things we're usually attached to. The confession and purification is an exercise in letting go of the negative or problematic things that we've done or experienced and are still holding on to. We think of all the negative actions we've done in this life and all our previous lives and we confess them; we feel regret and we resolve not to do them again. And then we feel that we let them go. We no longer hold on to any of these negative things. This is the essence of purification.

The fourth branch is *rejoicing*. Offering counters attachment, purification works on aversion and anger, and rejoicing works on jealousy and envy. Here we are rejoicing at the good things that other people have done or achieved. We think of all the good deeds achieved by the shravakas, the pratyekabuddhas, the bodhisattvas, the Buddhas, and all ordinary beings, and we rejoice. We feel happy about what they've done and we fully appreciate their goodness. Very often, when somebody does or receives something better than us, we're displeased. Here, on the contrary, we rejoice. This is also a very important practice that should be applied in our daily life.

The fifth branch is *'asking the Buddhas to turn the wheel of Dharma'* and the sixth is *'requesting them to live long and remain in this world'*. These branches are about appreciating the great value of the Dharma and wanting it to last and to spread far and wide. We ask the Buddhas to continue to give teachings and guidance to us and to all sentient beings, and also to live long. Teaching is the main activity through which a Buddha helps others, because that enables sentient beings to understand how to practise the Dharma and therefore how to help themselves.

The seventh and last branch is the *dedication*, which is a way of sharing the positive things that we have with all sentient beings. It is a reminder of our original bodhichitta motivation, of our wish and commitment to put an end to the sufferings of sentient beings and to lead them all, including ourselves of course, to the highest level of attainment, the highest level of peace. That is why we're practising. So, now that we've done some positive things, and have refrained a little from doing negative things, then whatever positive effects we've been able to gather we dedicate to all sentient beings; we pray that the whole result or fruit of these activities may ripen in each and every one of the countless beings throughout space. And we include in our dedication not only the positive effects of this particular practice but of all the positive things we've ever done in the past and even those we'll do in the future; we offer it all to all beings that they may benefit.

This Seven Branch Prayer is regarded as an important means to accumulate what we call 'merit'. Merit is accumulated through doing positive things or developing good habits. At first, it's important to eliminate our negative habits and exchange them for positive ones. Later, on a firm basis of positive habits, we may come to see the true reality, the way things really are, through which we will transcend all habits – even positive ones. That's how we can attain enlightenment. However we won't be able to do that if we don't work first on our negative patterns.

We should beware of getting too caught up with sophisticated philosophy, becoming fascinated by the 'high views' and 'high meditations' and overlooking this down-to-earth aspect of the practice. Some people only want to hear about, talk about and attempt to practise the highest teachings: Dzogpa Chenpo, Mahamudra, Zen satori, shunyata, Madhyamika, and they're so eloquent they can talk for hours about it – but they haven't changed in the least. They're prone to as much anger, pride and attachment as before. They may assert that there is nothing we can call 'I', and they can discourse on the subject, but if you slightly provoke them they flare up in anger. They're just ordinary people who've let this philosophy get into their heads so they've become all puffed up. They've become completely unbalanced with such big, inflated heads!

In Mahayana Buddhism we always find these two sides or facets, the relative and the ultimate, that have to go together in a balanced way. Merit and wisdom have to be developed simultaneously and support each other. The accumulation of merit helps us to develop positive habits that will create the favourable environment and circumstances for us to improve our understanding, meditation and realisation. Accumulation of merit thus contributes to the accumulation of wisdom. In turn, a deeper understanding and greater realisation of emptiness, of the true nature of reality, furthers the accomplishment of positive deeds because it reduces our clinging and selfishness. It's therefore essential to develop these two aspects in a balanced way.

OM　　MA　　NI　PAD　ME　HUNG

# Prayer for Liberating Beings from the Six Realms

We then recite the prayers for liberating beings from the six realms through Chenrezig's mantra.

As I explained in the beginning, this short Chenrezig practice was composed by Thangtong Gyalpo, who is regarded as the reincarnation of a nun called Gelongma Palmo who lived centuries ago in India. She was born as the daughter of a local king but when she got leprosy, she was expelled from the palace. She became a nun, a 'gelongma' or bhikshuni, and she intensively practised Chenrezig. Through her practice, she was able to heal herself and she became a great master. It is said that Thangtong Gyalpo composed this Chenrezig practice – and especially this prayer for liberating beings from the six realms – in remembrance of his past existence as Gelongma Palmo.

When we say the mantra, we visualise it at the heart of Chenrezig. In the centre of his heart, there's a white HRI ( ཧྲཱིཿ ), with the six syllables OM MANI PADME HUNG ( ཨོཾམཎིཔདྨེཧཱུྃ ) arranged around it. OM ( ཨོཾ ) is white, MA ( མ ) is green, NI ( ཎི ) is yellow, PAD ( པད ) light blue, ME ( མེ ) red and HUNG ( ཧཱུྃ ) is dark blue. These six syllables represent the 'six wisdoms' or the 'six Buddhas', who are in a way the six Buddhas of the six realms. Visualising them purifies specific emotions corresponding to the specific realms.

The syllable HUNG ( ཧཱུྃ ) is related to anger, hatred, our incapacity to forgive, our feelings of hurt, and all the emotions that come from anger and hatred. When the prayer mentions the hell beings, we feel that dark blue light radiates especially from the HUNG ( ཧཱུྃ ) and dispels all our negative emotions related to anger, hatred and hurtful feelings. And we also feel that this is happening to all the other sentient beings, that all their actions and emotions linked to anger, that would cause them to take rebirth in hell realms, are being completely pacified and purified by the light emitted by this letter HUNG ( ཧཱུྃ ). Feeling this, we say the mantra.

The prayer then mentions the 'hungry ghost realm', which is linked to strong clinging, intense attachment, miserliness, holding on to things without being able to share, give or even enjoy them. Such states of mind are the main cause for being born into the hungry ghost realm. When we recite the mantra, we particularly focus on the syllable ME ( མེ ) that radiates red light and dissolves or purifies – in ourselves as well as in all other beings – all the emotional states of strong clinging and miserliness that might cause us to be reborn as hungry ghosts. It closes the door to this realm for all beings.

The third realm, the animal realm, is associated with ignorance and related states of mind: dullness, not knowing, confusion and so forth. We feel that a very bright blue light radiates from the letter PAD ( པད ) and dissolves all our ignorance, dullness, obscurity and confusion, all our unknowing states. They're completely cleared in us and in all sentient beings. It prevents our being reborn in the animal realm and brings us wisdom and complete clarity.

The syllable NI ( ཉི ) is yellow. Its light dispels the sufferings of birth, sickness, old age, death and loss that are linked with the human realm. It completely purifies the desire, strong craving and attachment that are at the root of these sufferings, in ourselves as well as in all sentient beings, closing the door to unfortunate rebirth in the human realm.

The syllable MA ( མ ) is green and its light purifies whatever negative deeds we and all sentient beings throughout space may have done due to jealousy and envy. The causes and circumstances leading beings to take rebirth in the demi-gods realm are thus stopped and purified, and the negative emotions linked to it are transformed into the clear light of all-accomplishing wisdom.

The syllable OM (ॐ) is white and its light dissolves the pride and arrogance that are connected to the heavenly realms of the gods. Although the gods lead long lives of perfect pleasure and enjoyment, that might seem desirable to us, these sensual pleasures distract them from any concern about benefiting themselves or others. Not only are they not mindful of any necessity to practise, they are actually exhausting the positive results of their previous good karma. Even if gods live very long lives by human standards, they are not immortal, and the phase of decay preceding their death is very painful. Their foresight allows them to receive the unbearable vision of the miserable future existence awaiting them in lower realms. Therefore, when saying the mantra, we feel that a white light radiates from the syllable OM (ॐ) and purifies, in ourselves and others, all the manifestations of pride that might lead us to a rebirth in the god realm.

The sound of the mantra itself has a certain power. Akong Rinpoche did an experiment with dowsing once, when he was in Brussels. He switched the television on and stood in front of it with a dowsing rod. A dowsing rod twists violently when it comes across an electric current, and that's just what happened. He asked somebody to stand between the television set and the rod. The movement of the rod became even stronger because the person functioned as an electricity conductor. He then put a 'protection' on that person (some black pills from the Karmapa), and the rod stood still: the electricity was blocked and no longer passed through the person. He took off the protection, and again the electric current flowed through. This person was then asked to recite the OM MANI PADME HUNG mantra and, as with the protection, no electric current would pass through him. Such things happen!

The main power of the mantra comes, of course, from the dedication prayers of Chenrezig himself, but the power isn't just contained within the mantra. Its efficacy also depends on the person who recites it. It depends on how much trust and confidence the person has in this mantra and on that person's state of mind. If you're calm and concentrated, the mantra will be very much stronger than if you recite it with a distracted mind. And, of course, the mantra recitation of somebody whose mind is even clearer, who has reached a certain level of realisation, will be another hundred thousand times stronger. Like everything in this world, it depends on many factors. This is why we should try as much as possible to say this mantra in a meditative state. We should let our mind become calm and clear, and then, without tension, spaciously and peacefully, recite it.

The Tibetans usually repeat mantras while carrying on with their daily activities. They just keep the mala moving between their fingers and walk around, and when they meet somebody else, it's, "What are you doing?" "Oh, my neighbour is terrible!" And sometimes they don't even count the beads one by one, they count five or six together, going on with their conversation. One can recite mantras and do all kinds of things. However, if one wishes to say mantras properly, then the best way is to recite with the mind completely focused, without any distraction. Next best is to be distracted in a positive way, or to be distracted without thinking, but just feeling at ease and peaceful. The worst is to say mantras while being distracted in a negative way, like while being very angry. However, maybe – I don't know – it may be better to be angry and recite mantras than to be very negative without reciting mantras!

We should also, of course, recite it with a good aspiration, with bodhichitta, which is the bodhisattva's aspiration to benefit all sentient beings. We should trust that this mantra has come from Avalokiteshvara himself and that it carries all his blessings as well as those of all the great bodhisattvas and Buddhas of the past. We should recite it with full confidence, convinced that through its recitation we will really be able to help all sentient beings and ourselves. So we're working on the negative emotions of all sentient beings, while remaining ourselves in a clear and calm state of mind. We visualise and feel – feeling it is the main thing – that this is what happens to all sentient beings while we say the mantra.

The positive motivation with which one recites a mantra contributes to its efficacy. A story about Atisha Dipankara illustrates this. Atisha was a most learned Indian Pandit who was invited to Tibet in the 11th century. He developed a throat problem due to the harsh Tibetan climate and the altitude, and he couldn't get rid of the infection for a long time. Somebody mentioned a Tibetan who had helped many people by saying mantras, and Atisha agreed to see him. This Tibetan man was brought in, who recited the mantras very loudly, with very good intentions; but, because he was Tibetan, he didn't pronounce them properly. Atisha Dipankara was so bemused to hear the mantras pronounced in such a completely wrong way that he couldn't help laughing. He laughed and laughed, and he laughed so much that eventually the infectious blister in his throat burst open and he was cured!

There's another funny story about fake mantras. A man once asked a so-called lama to teach him a mantra. However, that lama was just posing as a lama and didn't actually know anything. The man was earnestly requesting a mantra and the fake lama didn't know what to say. Embarrassed, he looked around and saw a mouse appearing suddenly from a hole in the wall. He then said in Tibetan, "Pop up suddenly." He saw the mouse's whiskers and added, "It has whiskers." And then, as the mouse ran to and fro, searching and scratching around, he added, "It rummages here and there." Finally the mouse disappeared, so he said, "It disappears." And then, "There you are, that's the mantra."

The man thanked the fake lama and went away, reciting his freshly learnt mantra on the way. On his way home he had to travel through a dangerous place infested with robbers. He had to camp there for the night and he was terrified. Hoping the mantra would protect him, he recited it loudly. One of the robbers caught sight of him and decided to rob and kill him. The brigand slowly crawled to the tent. He was very near it when he heard a voice saying, "Pop up suddenly." Surprised, he thought the man was aware of his arrival. He stopped and listened more carefully. "It has whiskers." This thief had whiskers: he now really wondered whether the man knew of his presence. Then he started hunting about to see whether he could get hold of something outside the tent, and he heard, "He rummages here and there." By now, the thief was convinced that this man had special powers and knew about his presence and intentions. He was getting really scared and wondering what to do. Then he heard, "He disappears." So he ran away.

So the fake mantra worked quite well in a way. And of course the man who recited it had total confidence in his mantra and its efficacy.

# Self-Visualisation as Chenrezig

We now transform our own 'three doors', that is our body, speech and mind, into the deity's body, speech and mind. The text says:

> *De tar tse cik sol tap pe*
> *Phak pe ku le ö zer thrö*
> *Ma dak le nang thrul she jang*
> *Chi nö de wa cen gyi zhing*
> *Nang cü kye drö lü ngak sem*
> *Cenreziwang ku sung tuk*
> *Nang drak rik tong yer me gyur*

Having prayed to Chenrezig, who is in front of us or above us, we feel the light rays carrying his blessings and energy entering us and all sentient beings. All our defilements, all negativities, all the mind poisons are thus completely washed away and purified.

Buddhists believe that all the negative aspects of sentient beings are only temporary and 'acquired', like dust covering a clear crystal. When dust settles on a crystal it loses its clarity and transparency, but if you wipe off the dust it is again immediately clear and pure. The dust is not inherent to the crystal; it has not entered into its nature. We believe that the basic nature of our mind is pure awareness and clarity. It is the Buddha nature, identical to the nature of all the Buddhas. It is what we call our basic goodness. The negativity and defilement are not part of it; they are the result of a misunderstanding. There's nothing wrong with our actual nature; what's wrong is the way we perceive things. That's the problem. That's where all our problems – attachment, aversion, fear, dualistic views and all the rest – come from. So we don't have to do anything at the level of our own nature; we just need to change our way of looking.

All the negative emotions come from a basic misconception, a wrong perception that we call 'ignorance'. It's because of this wrong perception that all the negative aspects arise: the wrong habits and mistaken ways of reacting that generate destructive patterns and all our problems and sufferings. However, this 'ignorance' is just a mistaken way of seeing. There's nothing really wrong with the basis, with our actual situation. The problem is just due to a distorted way of seeing things and not to the way we actually are. It's the way we perceive things and how we're conditioned to react now, but it's not our true nature. So the mistake can be corrected – although it's not easy to do this. We're so used to this way of seeing that it's difficult for us to even imagine a state of being that would be different from the way we feel now. It's very difficult but it's not impossible.

All the practices are formulated on the basis of this fundamental understanding. However, this theoretical background is not explained in the sadhana itself, which functions not so much at an analytical level but rather at a more practical and experiential level. Therefore, here, we feel that through the blessings of Chenrezig and all the enlightened beings, our negative emotions, views, patterns and conditionings are being purified.

At the moment at which all the impure karmic appearances and delusions are completely purified, we become a Buddha. We have unveiled our basic pure nature, the Buddha nature, and we then perceive the outer world as

'Dewachen', the realm of Buddha Amitabha, and all the beings in that realm as Chenrezig or Drolma. Our own body takes the appearance of Chenrezig, our speech becomes his mantra and our thoughts are Chenrezig's thoughts of compassion and wisdom.

This is the Vajrayana way of practising: 'using the result as the path.' Of course, we can't totally understand or imagine what being Chenrezig feels like or what an enlightened being is thinking about, but through our studies and through our limited knowledge, we can imagine what it might be like.

We just become Chenrezig, almost as if we let our mind dissolve or mix with Chenrezig. We don't analyse this process; there's no place for thoughts, concepts and doubts. We just dissolve into Chenrezig, become Chenrezig, feel that Chenrezig and we have become one, and rest in that state. We let our mind 'be' Chenrezig and remain in this uncontrived nature of our mind.

'Uncontrived' is the important word here. We don't manipulate our mind. We just let it completely 'be', resting in the most open, most relaxed, most natural state. Then whatever we see is the union of emptiness and appearance together; whatever we hear is sound and emptiness together, and whatever we think is thought and emptiness together. Here emptiness means an absence of grasping. Whatever comes, we just let it be without grasping at anything. We just let things come and go.

This stage is what we call the self-visualisation: visualising ourselves as Chenrezig.

# Mantra Recitation

It is at this point that we can recite the mantra OM MANI PADME HUNG.

Inside Chenrezig, at the level of his heart, we visualise a letter HRI (ཧྲཱིཿ) standing on a flat moon disc floating above a lotus flower. It is three-dimensional. In the east, in front of this HRI (ཧྲཱིཿ), is the letter OM (ༀ). From the Buddhist point of view, the east is always the direction in front of the deity we visualise, so 'to the east of HRI (ཧྲཱིཿ) means in front of the HRI (ཧྲཱིཿ).

In the pictures, OM (ༀ) is usually represented above the HRI (ཧྲཱིཿ) because it's impossible to paint it in front without hiding the HRI (ཧྲཱིཿ). The OM (ༀ) should normally be facing inwards, that is towards the HRI (ཧྲཱིཿ). If I am the HRI (ཧྲཱིཿ), then I'll see the OM (ༀ) in front of me, not from the back but from the front. The other letters, MA (མ), NI (ཎི), PAD (པད), ME (མེ), HUNG (ཧཱུྃ) are arranged clock-wise around the HRI (ཧྲཱིཿ) and, if the mantra circles, it circles anti-clockwise. There are many meditations in which the letters of the mantra are moving, and when a mantra does move, it circles anti-clockwise. In this particular practice however there's no mention of moving letters: the mantra is not turning – it just shines without revolving.

Whether a mantra moves or not differs according to different visualisations in different sadhanas. It also depends on whether the main focus is on having the mind settle down or on integrating the movement of thoughts in the practice. If we want our mind to be very quiet and settled, then usually the mantra doesn't move. We don't even think about movement. However, most of the time our mind is very active and, in order to channel this movement, we can imagine that the mantra is revolving and radiating light. It integrates the activity into the meditation. Movement and immobility have different purposes and you don't have to be too rigid about it, I think.

We can alternate between different things, sometimes concentrating on the deity, on the presence of Chenrezig, sometimes on the mantra, sometimes visualising the syllables, sometimes just saying the mantra with our mind calm and relaxed without any particular focus, sometimes concentrating on the purification of our emotions and those of all sentient beings, on receiving the benefits and the healing. Sometimes we can focus on our own purification and healing, sometimes on the healing and the benefits we – as Chenrezig – bring to all sentient beings.

These are different things we can do alternately. We can concentrate on whichever aspect we want. However – and this is true for any mantra recitation – when we talk about 'concentration', that concentration shouldn't be too strong, too rigid, or too cerebral. We shouldn't let it happen only in our head, but rather get the feeling through our whole body; otherwise we'll get a headache!

During the first half of our mantra recitation, we can think about Chenrezig in front of us, and during the second half, we can concentrate on the purification process. That's the usual way, but what we actually do doesn't really matter that much. What kind of meditation or practice we do at this point actually depends on what kind of instructions we've already received, what level of practice we've reached.

A Mahamudra or a Dzogchen practitioner can apply that understanding, that type of practice and meditation here. If we have some understanding of the Madhyamika philosophy and the like, we can also use it here. If we don't have any such instructions or understanding, we can practice shinay: we just let our mind settle down and relax in the feeling that we have become Chenrezig, that we are one with him. These are different meditation methods that we can apply at this point.

If we are beginners, we can just say the OM MANI PADME HUNG mantra as a kind of prayer and feel that we receive energies and blessings that completely transform us.

We can also use the mantra in order to work on the six negative emotions and the six realms, for ourselves or for other people, in a similar way as during the 'Prayer for liberating beings from the Six Realms'. We visualise each of the syllables of the mantra with its specific colour preventing people from being born into the corresponding negative realms and helping them to free themselves from the related negative emotion. We then use the mantra as a liberating and healing medium.

As you can see, the same practice can be used at many different levels and this is true of whatever practice you're doing.

The mantra can be said in different ways. You can sing it, especially if you have a nice tune and a nice voice – otherwise you might drive your neighbours crazy! Singing it nicely can be very inspiring. You can also say it aloud, slowly and distinctly. There is another way that is compared in Tibetan to the 'buzzing of bees', of a beehive. You can also whisper the mantra or even say it in your mind, without any sound.

The sound of the mantra is considered to be very important. When a high-level practitioner reaches a stage of realisation that is called 'attaining the power of Dharani', he or she can create a mantra and empower its sounds with blessings.

We could compare the mantra to a code or password. If I give you my password for my computer, you can get into my e-mails, for instance. A mantra is something like a key that gives you access to the powers and qualities of the Buddha or bodhisattva who created it. If you have 'attained the Dharani', you can empower or bless a sound or sequence of sounds that becomes your mantra and has the power that you have. If I have a power, then my mantra has that same power and I create it so other people can use it and gain access to the qualities I have developed.

Because the sound is so important, mantras are not translated but are kept in Sanskrit. However, as you may have noticed, the same mantra sounds quite different when recited in Sanskrit with a Japanese, Tibetan, Thai, English, French or German accent. There are also many stories – like the one I just related – of mantras working quite well although recited all wrong. So how important is the sound really?

As I just mentioned, how powerful a mantra is depends on many things, not just on the sounds. It's better to pronounce it correctly, but the pronunciation alone is not all. I already mentioned that to say a mantra with good intentions is more important than to pronounce it correctly. And while it's generally thought that a correct pronunciation of a mantra gives it greater power, there are stories showing that a mantra said incorrectly can sometimes have more power than when said correctly.

Sakya Pandita, a Tibetan master who lived around the 12$^{th}$ century (1182-1251), was not only a great scholar but also a highly realised practitioner. Although he was never taught Sanskrit, it was the first language he could speak as a small child. He became a great Sanskrit scholar. He used to travel to India to debate with Indian philosophers and he converted many Hindus to Buddhism.

Once, as he was travelling from Tibet to India, he was passing through a dense forest. He could hear the sounds of mantras emanating from all over the place – from the trees, the rivers and the rocks. He thought that a great practitioner must be living nearby. However, the sound of the mantra he was hearing was not completely correct and he thought, "What a pity if this yogi is able to give such power to an incorrect mantra, how much more power it would have if he were saying it correctly." So he searched around to find the yogi. Having found him, he introduced himself, paid his respects, praised him for his great achievement and suggested that he pronounce the mantra in the right way.

"You're saying *'Om bendza chili chilaya'* whereas it's supposed to be *'Om vajra kili kilaya'*. You should change it."

The yogi then took his phurba, recited *'Om bendza chili chilaya,'* and struck a rock with the dagger. It went through the rock as if through butter. He turned to Sakya Pandita: "Now, please, you do the same with *kili kilaya!*" But Sakya Pandita did not try.

There are many stories like this one. I think you even have similar stories in Christianity. One such story lingers in my mind, although I don't remember the details. I think this story has been told by Tolstoy.

A bishop once visited three monks who lived on an island. The three monks were very happy to welcome the bishop. The bishop asked them what kind of prayers they were saying. The three men answered that they worshipped God from the bottom of their heart, but that the only prayer they knew was, 'You three, we three, please bless us!'

"Oh, no! That's not the right prayer. You must learn how to pray properly," exclaimed the bishop.

With great enthusiasm, the three monks begged him to teach them how to pray, "We're so grateful that you have come to teach us." Then the bishop taught them the Lord's Prayer: 'Our Father who art in Heaven...'

Unfortunately, it was very hard for the three men to learn it by heart. The bishop, who was a very nice person, patiently kept on repeating it and spent a long time teaching them until, at last, all of them could say the prayer nicely. Then he bid them farewell, went back to his boat and sailed away.

The next morning, as he stood on the deck, he saw three luminous points on the horizon; they seemed to be moving towards the boat. As they drew near, the bishop recognised the three monks, who were running on the waves. They were shouting, "Please, please, stop! Please tell us the prayer once more because we have forgotten."

Quite stunned, the bishop told them that he thought they no longer needed his prayer and that they could simply go on saying their own prayer, 'You three, we three, please bless us'. It seemed to be working just fine.

You can also think about or place the mind on the mantra in different ways. You can visualise all the letters of the mantra as white or see their respective different colours. You mainly visualise the six colours when you try to work on the different emotions and the six realms. Sometimes you can also imagine all the different, rainbow-like colours radiating from Chenrezig, from you and from the whole mantra.

You can repeat the mantra as many times as you wish: one, two, three, ten, twenty, a hundred malas; whatever. It only depends on the time you have.

When somebody does a Vajrayana practice, there are three kinds of criteria or standards to establish that this person has 'accomplished' the practice.

The best attainment is to actually gain a certain level of realisation, of real experience, from one's sadhana practice. So the best way is to practise until one gets such realisation. If that's not possible, a certain time limit is set. One does the practice for a certain length of time and one can then be regarded as somebody who has 'completed' that practice. That's second best. The third level of accomplishment is set by the amount of mantras one has recited. For each practice, there's a kind of 'minimum workable number' of mantras! The 'minimum number of mantras' for OM MANI PADME HUNG is what we call 'dru bum', which means we recite each syllable one hundred thousand times, multiply this by the number of syllables in the mantra, which makes 600,000 mantras in total. If one recites 600,000 mantras, one has completed the minimum mantra recitation and one is then supposed to be able to use this practice to help others as well. There is of course no guarantee that one has thus reached any level of realisation but it's a traditional way of assessing the average attainment of practitioners.

One counts the number of mantras with a mala. Usually, we hold the mala in our left hand, at the heart level, and we turn the beads between thumb and index towards us and when we come to the end of our mala, we turn it round. Not going over the 'end bead' may help us maintaining mindfulness; it indicates that we're aware that we have finished 108 mantras. But if you don't turn the mala round, I don't think anything bad will happen to you.

Some people prefer to recite mantras without a mala. Using a mala is usually a way of sustaining awareness. The mala itself is an object of awareness, like the breathing or any other object of meditation. If you're so concentrated and focused on the meditation that you don't need a mala, it's OK. But if you're not that good, then maybe the mala 'brings you back' sometimes. These things cannot be generalised and should be adapted to individual needs.

The objective of the practice is not to concentrate exclusively on one thing and keep only that one thing in mind. The aim is to develop a peaceful, calm state within which one is aware without distraction. One is still aware of everything that is going on and one is able to do many things. To be only aware of one single object is rather a test of concentration, like Arjuna's archery - this is a story from the Indian classic, the Mahabharata.

In this story, a great master had been teaching the Kauravas and the Pandava brothers to shoot arrows. He organised a test to determine who was his best student. He put a small clay figure of a bird in a tree and asked each of his students to aim at it. They were all very good shots.

"What can you see?" he asked the first one. "I see the leaves and the bird in the middle." The teacher did not let him shoot. He asked the same question to the next one. "I can see the bird, nothing else." He didn't let him shoot either. One of the strongest students said, "I can see just the head of the bird." He too was refused the opportunity to shoot. Finally, Arjuna's turn came.

"What can you see?" asked the master.

"I can see only the eye of the bird, nothing else."

"Now you shoot!" The arrow pierced the clay bird's eye, and Arjuna was proclaimed the best student.

When one is very concentrated, the mind is very focused and one sees only the object on which the mind is settled. This is good in the beginning, but it's not the whole thing. In meditation, one has to be aware of everything going on, of all the five senses open and reacting, but at the same time maintain the clarity and the calmness. In such a state, one should be able to do several things without getting distracted, for instance hold the mala and recite the mantra, and not only that but also play the damaru and the cymbals!

There are many instructions regarding the mala for instance how to bless it, how to visualise it, how to keep it nicely with some respect.

To bless the mala, we first read the Sanskrit alphabet and a certain mantra. Then we place our hands one over the other – like the sun and moon – around the mala, and we imagine that it dissolves. Then, the mantra appears out of nothingness in the form of the mala. The mala is no longer a material object but the garland of the mantra itself that circles between our fingers.

There are also descriptions of different types of malas. Some are supposed to be better than others for certain practices. For instance, malas made of bones are usually not used for the Chenrezig practice. Peaceful mantras are preferably recited with malas made of wood, seeds, precious or semi-precious stones. The seeds of the bodhi tree are supposed to be very good for malas.

There are actually many different Chenrezig mantras but this six-syllable mantra is the most popular and best known. Its meaning can be explained as follows.

OM (ॐ) may be considered as the origin of all sounds. Of course, it has also different meanings. For instance, the three sounds of which the syllable OM (ॐ) is made, 'A', 'O' and 'M', represent the three kayas. There are many possible interpretations but usually OM (ॐ) is regarded as the first sound or the origin of all sounds and therefore we find it at the beginning of almost every mantra.

MANI means the jewel, or wish-fulfilling jewel, and PADME, pronounced PEME by Tibetans, means the lotus flower. The combination of the two can mean either the jewel in the lotus or the lotus in the jewel. This is one of the names of Avalokiteshvara.

The MANI also symbolises compassion because, just as you can get whatever you want thanks to the wish-fulfilling jewel, compassion brings you the greatest benefit you could wish for. According to the Indian legends, there is, somewhere in this world, a very special blue gem that can grant you all your wishes. In order to get it, you must cross seven seas and, if lucky enough, after many trials, you'll arrive on an island in the middle of which stands a palace where the jewel is guarded by beautiful women. It's difficult to get in and even more difficult to get out! If, however, you succeed in getting this wish-fulfilling jewel, you should first wash it seven times with sea water, then wash it seven times with sweet water, then wipe it dry with silk and put it on top of a pole or banner. Then, if you pray and express a wish, first a little wind will clear the ground of any possible dirt, then a little rain will settle the dust, and finally whatever you wished for will fall from the sky. That's the legend.

The wish-fulfilling jewel represents compassion because compassion is what gives the best, most beneficial results for oneself as well as for others. Once we have compassion, we are automatically benefiting ourselves and others. This is why compassion is said to have the same quality as the wish-fulfilling jewel from which all good things come for all beings.

Wisdom is here represented by PADME, the lotus. The lotus is the symbol of cleanliness, of what is not stained, not spoiled. The lotus flower usually grows in muddy and sometimes quite dirty ponds but, when it blooms, the petals of the flower are always perfectly clean and unstained, even if it's blossoming in the middle of the most polluted, unclean area. This is why the image of the lotus represents purity, which also symbolises wisdom. Wisdom is synonymous with seeing the true nature of reality. When we understand the true nature of our mind and of all phenomena, then no defilement, no negativity, can stain or contaminate us.

MANI PADME are thus the symbols of compassion and wisdom that, like the two wings of a bird, should always be present simultaneously, complementing each other.

HUNG (ཧཱུྂ) is the syllable of the heart. It also means 'I am'.

The whole mantra thus means, 'I am the jewel in the lotus'. It reminds us of compassion and wisdom. When we say this mantra, our mind naturally goes to the essence of Chenrezig, which is unlimited compassion and wisdom in union.

Originally, these syllables were written in Sanskrit. As the Tibetans couldn't read Sanskrit, it was subsequently written in Tibetan script. Sometimes however, we still use the Sanskrit. You may wonder whether there's any reason for visualising the syllables in Tibetan or whether it's just a convention. It's of course possible to use the Roman alphabet to visualise the mantra but it would look quite different because more than one letter is then needed to represent one whole syllable. Personally, I think it's not that nice. Moreover, a great symbolical meaning is captured within their graphic representation. It's especially true of the letters OM (ༀ) and HUNG (ཧཱུྂ), which are very artistic letters. So I think it's better to stick to the Tibetan or Sanskrit script. If you find it difficult, why not forget about it 'being Tibetan' and just consider it as figures, as drawings?

There are only six letters: OM MA NI PAD ME HUNG – it shouldn't be too difficult to remember! I would advise you to look at a representation of Chenrezig and his mantra or to draw it yourself in order to memorize it more easily.

*The Commentary*

One should however understand that this visualisation is just a basis for the mind to settle down. It functions in the same way as when one is meditating on an object or on the breathing. The only difference is that the Vajrayana favours the choice of a pure enlightened being that functions as a basis to simultaneously settle the mind and develop positive tendencies. One thus works on two levels at the same time. This mantra recitation is the main part of the practice.

## Pure appearances

We've now come to the visualisation of ourselves and our whole environment as Chenrezig's body, speech and mind, which is what we call the 'pure vision' or 'pure perception'.

> *Dak zhen lü nang phak pe ku*
> *Dra drak yi ge druk pe yang*
> *Dren tok ye she chen pö long*

This means, our body and the bodies of all other beings become Chenrezig's body; all sounds are the six syllables; all thought activities are the great wisdom.

The 'pure vision' is a very important aspect of any Vajrayana practice and, as I already stressed earlier, visualising has more to do with feeling than with just 'seeing'.

Most of the meditation aspect of the practice is done during the mantra recitation and at this point here. When we practise in a group, the break for silent meditation is usually placed either here following the mantra recitation, or at the end when we have dissolved all appearances into emptiness. All appearances, the bodies of myself and others, are perceived as the form of Chenrezig, all sounds as his mantra, and all thoughts as the space of wisdom; and we remain in that 'enlightened state' for some time.

We should understand that this practice has two levels. The first corresponds to the perception or the feeling of an outer Chenrezig, existing outside of us. Then, through the influence and the blessings of this outer Chenrezig, we awaken our own inner Chenrezig – our own true nature – which is the second level of practice.

If we can carry a little of this understanding into our daily life, it can be of great benefit. When we understand that Chenrezig is actually the very essence of our being, and when we can maintain this awareness, we'll be able to visualise ourselves and others as Chenrezig, and to see our environment as his pure realm, hear sounds as his mantra and perceive our mental activities as Chenrezig's thoughts permeated with compassion and wisdom. This is what we call the integration: the integration of the practice into our daily life.

I think it also has to do with confidence. Mahayana Buddhism strongly emphasises confidence: the importance of not feeling discouraged, not belittling ourselves, not feeling incapable of achieving a great objective. Actually, a low self-esteem is regarded as one of the main obstacles on the Buddhist path and therefore self-esteem – which is a correct appreciation of our capacities – and confidence are very important qualities that we should develop.

Visualising ourselves as Chenrezig is part of this process. We can't have a low self esteem when we feel we are Chenrezig the bodhisattva, or a Buddha capable of liberating all sentient beings. Through this practice we acknowledge that, at least, this possibility exists and that there's no difference in nature between a Buddha and ourselves. We all have the same potential and basic capacities as the Buddha to work on ourselves and to benefit other beings. We all have the Buddha nature; we all belong to the same 'caste', what we call 'rig' in Tibetan. This word can be translated as 'potential', but the literal meaning rather denotes a lineage, belonging to a certain family, race or caste. The son of the king has the 'rig' of the king. If you are born as the son of a king, you have the natural right to become a king. In the same way, being born as a human being, we have the 'Buddha rig', the natural birthright to become a Buddha. So, why not? Why not!

I used to say "Why not?" A lot. Some ten years ago, the college where I was teaching in Sikkim appointed me as co-ordinator of cultural activities. My colleagues joked, "We should call this appointment 'Why not?'" I accepted the post on condition that they would let me do whatever I wanted and I told my students that I was leaving them a clear field to do whatever they wished. They first suggested a music evening with live bands and such kinds of festivities. I said, "OK, why not?" After this, they proposed to organise a fashion show. I said, "OK, why not?" And then they wanted a beauty contest. It went on for several days but I was disappointed by the beauty contest because they didn't select the most beautiful but the most intelligent girls – and the winner was actually the least beautiful of them all! They argued that she was the best talker and that selection was based on such criteria in all beauty contests. I disagreed, explaining that organisers first select the most beautiful girls and only then ask questions to find out the one who has intelligence on top of beauty. But I lost the argument. But this is just a digression.

It's very important to have confidence in our potential. Feeling that all the blessings, all the positive energies are really penetrating us and all other sentient beings, this corresponds to the healing, the purification aspect of the practice. We are also generating compassion for ourselves. It is more or less the basis of all the healing methods that we find in the different spiritual and therapeutic systems. If we do it with a certain degree of confidence, I think it can be very helpful for ourselves and maybe for others as well.

We should try to remember and use this technique as often as possible. Usually, when we feel good, when everything goes all right, we don't find it difficult to sit on our meditation cushion and do our practice nicely. But when we encounter some trouble or problem, we get so upset that we can't do our practice any more. If this is the case, our practice is actually no use. The practice is in fact meant to help us work on our problems. It's precisely in times of troubles that we need it most. Then we should practise more often and more strongly and feel these things that I have just described.

It doesn't matter if we don't feel much in the beginning but we should at least try to focus our mind when we say the mantra. That is also how we work on the six types of emotions connected with the six realms in our everyday life. Whenever a negative emotion comes up, we immediately use the mantra and the visualisation, concentrating more specifically on the letter and the colour connected to the particular negative emotion that we experience, and we feel that it dissolves. This interrupts the flow of negative emotion that surges within us, in a very simple and practical way.

If we understand the underlying philosophy, what we call the 'view' of emptiness, the true nature of the mind and of all phenomena, then it's even better because it gives greater power to our practice. However, even if we don't understand the nature of the mind, we can at least apply this simple technique.

If a strong negative emotion arises in the mind, for instance we feel very angry, sad or hurt, at that very moment we just think of Chenrezig, feel his compassion and wisdom, and concentrate on the mantra, especially on the letter HUNG (ཧཱུྂ) and its radiance. In this way, we directly work on our emotions in a feeling way, not just intellectually. Moreover, this is something we can do anywhere and at any time. It's not necessary to go through the whole text of the sadhana from beginning to end; we just use the mantra and the visualisation wherever we are.

We can also use this method when we try to help others. We can visualise the mantra and its lights radiating and completely healing a person who's in trouble, sick, dying or dead. It is similar to the *Tonglen* practice but easier in a way, because we don't have to take the other person's problems on ourselves and help him or her on our own but instead we can help others through the power of Chenrezig and all the enlightened beings.

One doesn't have to be a Buddhist and believe in Chenrezig in order to apply this method. We are talking here about any positive energy that is present and can be felt. Such positive energy is not linked to a particular faith or belief. You can invoke whatever inspires you most, whatever you think of as most positive, and just try to keep feeling its flow: you feel cared for and you receive constant love and compassionate attention.

This is the main characteristic of Vajrayana practices: whether we are awake or asleep, even when we are dreaming, we try to get more and more accustomed to our positive support – in this case, Chenrezig. The dream is usually considered as the 'test' of our practice. If we are dreaming, especially if we have a nightmare, and we can feel Chenrezig's presence, or if we can visualise ourselves as Chenrezig and maybe radiate light and transform the nightmare into a peaceful dream, it means that we are really accustomed to that practice. It is said that if we can do this, we'll have no problem at the time of death. When death comes, during the frightful bardo time, we'll remember this practice and avoid being panic-stricken. In the bardo, we are just a mental body with no physical anchor and therefore whatever practice we can remember at that time becomes much more powerful. We may even be liberated during the bardo.

When our mind focuses on the Lord of Compassion, the embodiment of compassion and loving kindness, then whatever state of mind was previously ours is naturally transformed into a positive state of mind. That's the main understanding here. It is also believed that even when we do a simple shinay meditation, our meditation is more powerful if we visualise ourselves as a deity because it lessens our usual grasping at our self-identity, at the person we rigidly think we are, and at the same time it gives our mind a pure focus.

Any type of meditation, be it shinay or lhakthong, is of course a way of working on our negative emotions. Actually, we've nothing else to do on the whole Buddhist path except to work on negative emotions. Everything, every practice, is somehow a way of doing just that. With the shinay or shamatha meditation, we learn how to let our mind relax in whatever comes up. We just let things come and go, keeping our mind undisturbed, calm and wakeful in the present moment. That's the essence of the shinay meditation.

When our mind has gained greater calm – which does not mean that we keep it pressed down and locked in a box but, on the contrary, that we let it be spacious, vast as space – then things can arise freely and flow by. In the space of the sky, winds can blow, rain can fall, and clouds of all shapes and colours can move around without affecting the sky in any way. If we let our mind be as spacious as the sky, emotions and thoughts of any kind can come and go without generating any fear or concern. We don't grasp at them, we don't struggle with them, and they naturally dissolve. Sometimes we use the example of the sea and the waves. The waves come and go but they're not separate from the sea. They're not 'disturbing' the sea. They are neither bad nor good for the sea. Waves are just phenomena. If we can take our own mental 'arisings', whatever comes and goes, in the same way, then we can find peace of mind. That is most important to learn!

Vipashyana or lhakthong practice means trying to look at the thoughts and emotions at the very moment of their arising. The very moment something comes up, we look at it. When I use the verb 'to look at', it doesn't mean that we are actually 'looking' as if we were looking at an object. We don't transform the arising into an object that we investigate from outside: "This is the anger!" It's rather a process of looking from within. That thought, that consciousness or that emotion is itself an aspect of our mind. It is our own mind's arising, nothing else. We should talk of looking 'in' rather than looking 'at'. We just face it – although 'facing it' may not be the best expression either.

We should just 'let be' within it. 'Within' does not mean that we have to go inside something; it's just that we relax within it.

And within that emotion, thought or whatever, at that very moment, we may find that there is nothing to grasp. This is not a conceptual but an experiential way of understanding the nature of our mind. Finding nothing we can grasp, nothing we can pinpoint or really work on, we just let our mind 'be' in that state, moment by moment, whatever may come. We're just aware: 'aware within' rather than 'aware of something'.

When we rest in that state, we gain the confidence of knowing that there's nothing beyond our control. We've nothing to fear because nothing can harm us; everything is just right. This is all there is, there's nothing else and that's the way it is. Things come up and disappear like everything else - nothing remains, so there's nothing to hold onto. That's the nature of mind! Sometimes it is described as 'unborn' and 'unceasing'. Nothing is quite real or truly existing, so there's nothing that can finish, either.

We let our mind merge into Chenrezig's essence, into the state of mind of all enlightened beings, and we feel completely relaxed and free. That's the core of the meditation.

Of course, this has much to do with the understanding of emptiness and selflessness. I will not enter into this subject now; it's not easy to explain and it would require more time than we have available.

# The Dissolution

At the end of the practice, we dissolve the visualisation. These two phases of creation and dissolution of the visualisation are two important parts of the practice. First, Chenrezig arises in front of us and the people around us and we become Chenrezig and our surroundings appear as his pure land. In the second phase, our environment, the beings around us, and even ourselves as Chenrezig, all dissolve into nothingness.

Everything disappears and becomes completely empty, void. Nothing remains. This is not the emptiness of the shunyata philosophy, it's just the disappearance of whatever we had previously mentally created. We take a break here to let our mind remain in this open, natural, non-grasping state.

We can actually have breaks anywhere when we practise alone. It's good to pause and place the mind in its 'natural state' whenever we feel appropriate. However, when we practise in a group, the break is usually placed either here, when we have dissolved all appearances into emptiness, or earlier, before the beginning of this section, after the mantra.

# Re-emergence and Dedication

At last, from this void, we appear again as Chenrezig and, within the awareness of being Chenrezig, we say the dedication prayer.

In all the Mahayana and Vajrayana practices we have three sacred stages: the aspiration, the actual practice inspired by the understanding of the true nature, and the dedication.

At the end of any practice we dedicate the merit, which actually only differs from the initial bodhisattva's aspiration in its formulation. The aspiration prayer expresses our wish to start to practise for the benefit of all sentient beings, whereas in the dedication we pray that whatever positive energy, positive results or positive karma we may have gained through the practise we've done, be dedicated towards the objectives stated in our initial aspiration prayer.

We not only dedicate the positive results generated by this particular session of practise but by all the positive deeds we ever did in the past as well as all the good things we will do in the future. We dedicate not only for the benefit of all the sentient beings collectively but for each individual being as well. We express the wish that each and every individual being throughout space may get the full benefit of the full result of all our positive deeds.

So we say the prayer:

> *Ge wa di yi nyur du dak*
> *Cen re zi wang drup gyur ne*
> *Dro wa cig kyang ma lü pa*
> *De yi sa la gö par shok*

This means, 'By the virtue of this practice and all the other practices that I have done, may I attain the state of Chenrezig, the Lord of Compassion, and may I then be able to bring all the sentient beings to that same state, even if I myself have to do it all alone'.

That's the courageous compassionate attitude of a bodhisattva, who is ready and willing to undertake the mission alone if necessary. If he receives help, that's good, but if no one helps him, it doesn't matter. His determination doesn't weaken even if nobody appreciates what he is doing. He's not looking for appreciation, fame or popularity. He doesn't expect people's encouragement, gratefulness, or praise. He simply does what he has decided to do.

# Additional Prayers and Phowa

After the dedication, we say all the other prayers we wish to add.

We usually recite the Dewachen prayer, especially when we do the practice for other people or for people who have died. It's at this point that we can add a short phowa, or transference of consciousness, practice.

We think of the person for whom we want to do the phowa and we visualise his or her consciousness as a small letter HRI (ཧྲཱིཿ). We concentrate on that letter and, through the power of our mind, we 'catapult' it, forcefully sending it off as if it were a rocket, into Amitabha's pure realm, or into Amitabha's or Chenrezig's heart, where it mixes with the letter HRI (ཧྲཱིཿ) in the deity's heart. We then feel that this person becomes inseparable from Amitabha or Chenrezig. We can repeat this visualisation several times.

If the body of the dead person is beside us, we can visualise the HRI (ཧྲཱིཿ) within the person's body, but if the body is not there, we just concentrate on the letter HRI (ཧྲཱིཿ) with the conviction that this HRI (ཧྲཱིཿ) is the dead person's consciousness. If we're doing it for ourselves when we are dying, we visualise our own consciousness as the letter HRI (ཧྲཱིཿ) at the level of our heart, and we send it up through the central channel and transfer it into Amitabha's or Chenrezig's heart in the same way. The phowa should only be done after somebody is dead. One can start immediately after death or do it a long time after the person died; it doesn't matter.

We shouldn't spend too much time on this phowa section of the practice. The best thing we can do for a person who has died is the Chenrezig practice itself and it is only at the end of it that we can spend a few minutes to do this phowa. If we wish to help someone who's dying and can't do a formal practice because of the circumstances (if we're working for instance), we can still recite mantras mentally, and we can certainly develop a benevolent attitude towards that person and pray for him or her. We can of course also do the same for an animal.

This Chenrezig sadhana can be done in different ways. We can make it more or less elaborate depending on the time we can devote to our practice.

For instance, we can start with a lineage prayer if we want, before we start the actual practice, but if we don't have time, it's not necessary to do it; the practice is still complete even if we don't say a lineage prayer. The main practice starts from the refuge prayer and ends with the dedication.

One can include or omit the seven branch practice and/or the prayer for liberating beings from the six samsaric realms. If we have only little time, we can just skip them and, after the four lines of praise to Chenrezig, go directly to the self-visualisation.

Recitation of the mantra OM MANI PADME HUNG is essential, as well as the rest of the practice until and including the dedication. That is a must. However the Dewachen prayer is not absolutely necessary: we can do it once, three times, or more if we wish, but we can also not do it at all. The practice remains complete without it. We can also add whatever extra prayers or dedications we wish to recite to conclude the practice.

In this particular text we find a short Guru Rinpoche practice, which is something totally different. Guru Rinpoche is regarded as an emanation of Avalokiteshvara. The Tibetans regard him as, at the same time, the most important patriarch who brought Buddhism to Tibet and a very powerful bodhisattva who is especially active and helpful in dark, degenerated periods like ours. This is why people practice Guru Rinpoche – and we can do it also, if we wish and if we have the time, but it's not part of the Chenrezig practice and it's not absolutely necessary.

The Chenrezig sadhanas are countless. They were the first sadhanas to be introduced in Tibet. The *Mani Kambum* comprises two big volumes containing everything about the Chenrezig practices. It's supposed to have been written by King Songtsen Gampo and it contains a great many Chenrezig practices. Moreover, over the centuries, many other practices have been introduced from India and many have been created in Tibet. There have also been many Chenrezig *termas*. Every 'treasure-finder' has a Chenrezig practice.

Some of the practices are long; some are short; some are more elaborate. Chenrezig can take different forms: there are red, white, blue, yellow, black, Four-armed, Eleven-armed, One Thousand-armed, wrathful or peaceful forms of Chenrezig. According to the specific sadhanas, Chenrezig is sometimes visualised in the heart, sometimes above the head. Sometimes one visualises only one, sometimes many Chenrezigs; sometimes different aspects of Chenrezig are visualised inside every chakra inside the body. Sometimes one is supposed to visualise a Thousand-armed Chenrezig with a Four-armed Chenrezig in his heart, within whose heart is a Two-armed Chenrezig or another Four-armed Chenrezig. There can be so many different ways; all are possible. Actually, they are not basically different from one another. The One Thousand-armed Chenrezig is not 'the aspect of Chenrezig that we visualise outside', as opposed to a Four-armed Chenrezig who would be 'the aspect that we visualise inside'. There's nothing like that. The visualisation process is similar for any aspect of the deity. All these practices are in essence the same. If we know this, whatever the practice we do, it won't be a source of confusion.

Whenever one does a particular sadhana, one should visualise the form described in that particular text because there's some purpose for it, but at the same time one should understand that this particular visualisation is the embodiment of all the enlightened beings. Within it, one should include all the Buddhas and bodhisattvas, the whole lineage of great masters, the spiritual teacher and the essence of all the positive energies. They are all present in that one embodiment. Whatever practice one does, this is the very essential point to understand.

## Conclusion: The Devotional Approach

In Buddhism, we find many different levels of teachings and practices. They're all guidelines and instructions to help us understand and experience our true nature. Some are very deep and profound, and rely on understanding and wisdom. However, there are different types of people and those who are more devotional can also approach the path in a devotional way. This devotional approach has its own purposes and its own benefits.

I think it's important to concentrate on the letter HRI (ཧྲཱིཿ) and, through the power of our mind, we 'catapult' it, forcefully sending compassion and wisdom out to all beings. This is the approach that I've been trying to introduce here. I believe that prayer and devotion are part of all spiritual traditions throughout the world and, although Buddhism is a non-theistic religion – it doesn't believe in a creator, in a God standing somewhere above the creation – it still believes in the effectiveness of devotion and prayers as well as in grace and blessings. They are indeed effective ways of working on ourselves.

It's helpful to know how to pray. It's not easy and it's becoming more and more unfamiliar, especially in the West, although devotional prayers have been a very strong tradition in the Christian faith. We should understand that praying has nothing to do with blind faith. If we know how to pray, it's a natural thing to do: we are opening our mind.

There's always something deeper than what we ordinarily see or understand, a deeper level beyond what is apparent. We should remember it and be aware that there are beings who are more advanced than we are, who have more realisation than we do. Their very existence shows us that a more enlightened state of mind is possible, that more compassion and more wisdom are achievable. We may then understand that there is a possibility to receive their inspiration, to open up to their influence.

Praying is a powerful way of finding some security. It's actually a way of 'letting go' and it can be very helpful sometimes. Through praying, we accept that whatever has to happen will happen; we do our best, we pray, we dedicate whatever good things we did or have, and then we let things happen, let things be. To be able to pray like this denotes a very deep sense of letting go. We no longer feel anxious; we don't struggle any more. Instead, we trust – or even if we can't be totally trusting, at least we accept.

For me, it's a little like flying in an airplane. When you get into an airplane, you know it's quite possible that you won't come down – or rather that you will come down, but not necessarily alive! This awareness leads some people to panic or get drunk but, however much you panic and however drunk you get, if the plane has to crash, it will crash. Fear is useless because it won't save anybody's life. Why not accept the inevitability of the situation? So I say to myself, "OK, I'm on this plane now. I have no choice. I'll have to die one day anyway, so if I have to die today in this airplane, well that's OK, that's what was meant to be." And then I peacefully go to sleep. If I'm lucky, the plane will land safely. And if I'm not, I will die in my sleep, which is much better than being awake and panic-stricken.

This is the attitude of prayer that I want to convey, this sense of trusting ourselves to whatever may happen. We pray for the best, we do as many positive things as we can, but then we let it be. If the worst has to happen, let it happen. With such an attitude, we are less afraid, and we don't panic, because we are prepared for the worst.

Trust doesn't mean that we're a hundred percent sure that our plane will not crash and that nothing will ever go wrong. One can never be a hundred percent sure of anything. Trust means that we are confident that we did whatever we had to do and that whatever happens next is what was meant to be. That kind of trust, that sense of prayer, makes life easier. We lead our life with less struggle, tension and confusion, in a more relaxed way.

Indeed, whatever has to happen will happen anyway. Of course, it doesn't mean that we just walk along with our eyes closed and fall into the ditch, but that we deeply understand that there are certain things we can do and certain things we can't. One can never have total control of any situation. Knowing that, we should try our best to secure a positive outcome but still keep this sense of letting go, of trusting – and relax within it. This is something important to develop because it will help us to become happier, more relaxed and less insecure, less anxious, less confused and undecided.

Of course, if we can simultaneously work on our mind, and on our emotions, that's the real practice, the real self-development, and if, on top of that, we can go deeper inside and see the true nature of our mind, it's even better. We have then reached a stronger and higher level of practice.

However, we shouldn't worry if we can't do all that. We are beginners just starting our journey and we have to acknowledge that we have many things to learn. It's not expected that we understand everything from the moment we hear or read the teachings and start to practise. It's not possible and it's not what is expected of us.

Sometimes, when we listen to very clear teachings or read very good books, certain ideas, certain concepts develop in our minds and we think we've really understood something. However, this is only a limited and superficial understanding that needs to be worked on. We have to dig deeper and deeper until we get to the actual experience that is the real understanding. It's not easy, and it takes a long time.

Sometimes even the simplest things take a long time to really understand. Actually it's precisely the simplest things that take the longest time to learn. For instance, when giving meditation instructions, we talk about the 'uncontrived mind'. 'Uncontrived mind' is very easy to say: it's just 'not contrived'. But it's much harder to know what it refers to! It may take years and even decades just to get to know what is actually meant by this word! It is not something that one can immediately understand. Of course, one can't generalise, and there are people who immediately understand, but they are rare and exceptional individuals. We should know this and thus avoid impatience and discouragement.

To conclude, the last remark I would like to make is that what we practise is not really important. Some people think that they need to practise this first and that after, and wonder what they should do next. This is not the right approach. "What's next?" is not important. What matters is not what we practise but how we practise – how deeply we can go into it and how much we understand from deep down, from the heart. That is very important. I am totally convinced that somebody can become enlightened just by doing this short Chenrezig practice. We don't need anything else: everything is actually there, but we need to work on it. We need to go deeper into it, to actualise it, to integrate it into our real experience. Practice is not doing different things but going deeper into things. And by this, I don't mean going deeper into the text but into ourselves.

Of course, it doesn't mean that one shouldn't do anything else or get any other teachings than these. That's not what I mean. On the contrary, we should get many teachings from different sources and we should study as much and as widely as we can, but each of these teachings should bring us some deeper understanding of our main practice.

If we take Chenrezig or any other practice as our main practice, whatever experiences we go through, whatever we understand through our studies, whatever meditations and techniques we learn, should all help us gain a deeper understanding and experience of our own main practice. There's no need to change from one practice to another: all we need is to get a deeper understanding of the one practice we have chosen.

This is important to understand because, as I have repeatedly stressed, Dharma practice is actually nothing but working on ourselves. All the different techniques and methods are just means to help us do that! We have to discover them, learn them and then apply them and integrate them into our own experience.

# DISCUSSION

**QUESTION:** It's difficult for me to visualise the moon disc and I think this is because I don't understand its meaning. Why do we visualise a moon disc? If it just remains an empty shape, nothing more, nothing will arise from it.

**RINGU TULKU RINPOCHE:** The moon and the sun have great significance, especially in the old, traditional cultures. The moon and sun generally represent male and female energies. But for the moment we can keep to a basic understanding without going too much into a deeper meaning. Just think of a very small round flat disc. It is neither white nor yellow, it's the colour of the moon, nicely shining but not too bright. Let's not go deeper than that, just the shape.

**Q:** Rinpoche, I may be wrong but I think what would help me visualise might precisely be some deeper understanding of its significance

**RINPOCHE:** Usually, when we visualise these moon and sun discs supporting the mantra, it's in the context of a complex sadhana through which we are actually working on our experience of life and death. The main purpose in Vajrayana is working on our habitual tendencies. Among our habitual tendencies, the roughest and most solid level is our body, our 'form'. After this comes our speech and verbal concepts, then our thoughts and emotions, and finally our more subtle consciousness. If we really want to transform ourselves we have to work on all four levels. We particularly have to work on our birth and death experiences, as they are our most traumatic ones. This is true for everybody. If we don't work on our birth and death experiences, we won't be able to get rid of our fear. It is precisely in order to work in a painless way on our experiences of birth and death that we do these visualisations in the sadhanas.

First we visualise that everything is empty. Then there suddenly appears a lotus flower, a sun disc and a moon disc. They represent the basis of our existence, namely the coming together of the father essence and the mother essence. Then our mind, or consciousness, drops on to the sun and moon discs in the form of a letter, like HUNG or OM. Then this syllable transforms into the deity of the sadhana we are practising. This corresponds to our birth. We feel we are being born.

After that, all the prayers, offerings, mantra recitations and practices correspond to the daily activities that fill up our lives. And at the end everything dissolves progressively, both our environment and ourselves. That corresponds to dying and the different stages of dissolution. Afterwards, we arise again as the deity.

We thus go through the experience of appearing and disappearing. That's why we call it 'creation and dissolution'. It actually means working on our experience of birth, life and death. There are of course many different aspects, many different levels in it, but that's the main understanding.

However, this short Chenrezig practice is very simple and does not develop this long and complex process. We visualise Chenrezig in front of us, as a source of loving kindness and compassion. The point is to feel the compassion and wisdom of another being towards us in order to develop it in ourselves. I think it is important because, as is clearly understood nowadays, somebody who's never received love is likely to have psychological problems and to have difficulty feeling love for others. It's necessary to receive loving kindness in order to be able to give it to others. This is precisely what we are receiving here. We don't necessarily need to receive it only from our mother or father. Why resent our parents for not having loved us enough? Why not receive it directly from the greatest, kindest and most loving enlightened being, from the very source and embodiment of love and compassion himself?

**Q:** Why has this never been explained to me? I am surprised because I think it's quite important and, for I don't know how many years, I never heard such an explanation about the meaning of sadhanas. I don't understand this.

**Rinpoche:** Well, there are many things that have not yet been explained to you! Actually, this is the core of the Vajrayana sadhanas. You can find explanations in many texts and commentaries but here we are not going through the text of a long and complex sadhana that would justify such an explanation. We also haven't gone through such explanations so far because of a lack of time.

**Q:** I am surprised that there is time enough to practise but not to explain?

**Q:** I feel as surprised as she is. When I first came to a Dharma centre, people just told me to do a certain practice because it was good for beginners, without any further explanation. I did it, but I stopped after a while because I didn't understand what I was doing and why I should do it. As I'm not born as a Buddhist, I don't have the deep trust that would allow me to do something without understanding why. Therefore I think it's very important to get information on sadhanas, as you just gave us.

**RINPOCHE:** I certainly think it is important to get a deeper understanding of the meaning of a sadhana. However, this Chenrezig sadhana is too simple for us to go through all these explanations. Maybe some other time, if I explain a complex sadhana, I'll follow a commentary and we'll see all this in detail. There are actually so many things to explain!

We generally talk about four levels: the 'form' level, the 'speech' level – which has a wider scope than just verbal expression and words; it also encompasses concepts – then the 'mind' level of emotions and feelings, and finally a more subtle, 'subconscious' level. It's because we have to work on these four levels that we find such four-fold classifications as the four kayas and the four bardos. And there are many different ways of working on them.

For instance, colour is important, because colour is the basis of all forms. All forms are coming from colours and lights in a way – you can call it 'energy'. When we are working with colours, we are actually working with many different aspects – emotions, for instance, among other things.

The chakras and subtle channels are also important. What we call chakras are actually just strategic points of our subtle nerve system. If we focus our attention on a certain point, all our energy goes to it and starts working there. Even modern science has discovered that mental concentration on certain important glands, like the thyroid and thymus, affects their functioning. The same happens with the chakras, which is why we are taught certain techniques to work on them.

The breathing is also important.

These are all ways of working with the body and mind together, because body and mind aren't two completely separate entities. We can work on the mind through working on the body, but even more important in a way is to work on the body through the mind. If we can make our mind more relaxed and peaceful, and avoid being too tight or too stressed, then also, everything goes in the right direction. This is the purpose of meditation, and this is simpler to explain and to understand.

When I talk about 'mind', I do not restrict the meaning of this word to the thinking mind, but I give it a broader meaning, including the whole of our experience, the totality of what controls our body, heart and head all together in a way.

Letting our mind relax means that we gain some confidence in our ability to let whatever manifests – good or bad experiences, any kind of emotion – come and go. That's the most important thing, because then we know that whatever happens is manageable. We can deal with any occurrence, because we can let it come and let it go. Nothing is a threat any more.

There are two categories of meditation practices, shamatha and vipashyana. The purpose of the shamatha meditation is to make our mind calm and clear;

nothing else. The objective of vipashyana meditation is to directly see the nature of our mind, to clear our ignorance.

We usually start training in meditation with shamatha, because it's easier than vipashyana. In shamatha meditation, we try to let our mind simply 'be', without falling prey to distraction or dullness. We keep it peaceful and aware, and don't allow it to be overpowered by the five senses. The technique is to sit in the right posture and just let our mind rest at ease and relaxed in the present moment. Shamatha meditation doesn't require finding a place where there's absolutely no sound. Actually, it's impossible to find such a place, and even if there were a place where there's absolutely no sound, one would still be disturbed by all the sounds produced within one's own body. The point is not trying to get rid of disturbing sounds but trying to develop a state of mind in which sounds do not disturb our meditation. Shamatha meditation means developing an inner strength, a mental stability that prevents our mind being carried away by whatever happens, be it sounds, sights or smells. Sounds are actually the 'test' of meditation.

Vipashyana covers many different things. We could categorise it into an analytical and a non-analytical approach. The main objective of vipashyana is trying to find the truth, to see how things really are. One way of doing this is to analyse things, to see with the mind's eye how things are and analyse them in a more precise, minute and detailed way.

The non-analytical approach has many levels. The starting point of vipashyana meditation is the development of mindfulness. We talk for instance about what we call the 'four mindfulnesses': mindfulness of body, feelings, mind, and phenomena. We let our mind relax and settle in calm and peacefulness – which is shamatha meditation – and, of course, within that state, thoughts come up. When they do, we let them come up and go. We just 'look' at that momentary thought. Who are we actually? This is in fact our main search. Who are we? What is it that we call 'me'? We come to realize that we are what we think. Aren't our thoughts, our experiences, what we call 'me'? Or can we identify anything different? Basically, our consciousness, our thoughts, feelings and emotions are what make us think, 'I am'. In this way, we try to look at ourselves, to look at our mind. We may then find out that we cannot 'look at our mind'. What is our mind? Is it long, broad, soft, red? Our mind is not a 'thing'; our mind is 'now'. Our mind is this thought, this thought, this thought! The vipashyana technique is to be aware of these occurrences moment by moment. Realising the instantaneous nature of this process will lead us to understand more clearly who we are.

Later on, of course, vipashyana and shamatha are no longer separate from one another. Vipashyana and shamatha are ways of working on ourselves and not two different things. Shamatha is used as a means, a method or a basis to help us find our true nature, because we will not be able to see it unless we can be free from distraction and dullness. If our mind is too busy, too confused, we will be unable to see what is going on at a more subtle level.

Shamatha meditation is all about relaxing. Relaxation is the most important thing; not concentration. It depends of course what one exactly means by 'concentration'. For some people, 'concentration' can be a tense and rigid process, a source of tension that will actually generate more thoughts and distractions.

The best approach to meditation is to relax physically as well as mentally. This is important, because some people try to relax the mind by concentrating in the head only and they are surprised to get headaches. We should relax completely, body and mind. We put the body and mind at ease, not concentrating, but at ease, completely peaceful, without tensions. Then there will be less going on. Of course, we'll still perceive what goes on around us. We aren't shutting off our senses and our body – we wouldn't be able to do that anyway – and our mind is as restless as ever, running after any sound, smell or sight. But when that happens, we just keep aware of what is going on.

Awareness and mindfulness are the only tools we have when we meditate, be it vipashyana or shamatha meditation. When we are aware of what is happening, when we know that we've gone off shopping somewhere, then we just remember where we actually are and what we are currently doing. To do this, we may need some support to focus our awareness, like the breathing or some other object, whether mental, imaginary or real. We let the mind settle on that object. Let the mind be aware of the object, but not too concentrated, just lightly settled on it. That's the technique.

We keep on doing this. Whenever we notice our mind has escaped, we just bring it back. To 'bring it back' is not a forceful process. We don't have to make an effort. Efforts bring tension. It simply means remembering one thing: 'here, now', and our mind is automatically here.

And we should of course avoid dullness as much as distraction. Sleeping is not meditating. I am an expert at that!

**Q:** How can I develop faith in the fact that the positive energy I visualise emanating from Chenrezig actually reaches and helps all sentient beings? It's difficult for me to imagine that this is really happening. Moreover, as a beginner, I don't even try to think and imagine all sentient beings, but I rather visualise the people I know, those who are close to me – my family and friends. But then I have doubts as to how my relatives would actually receive this energy because I didn't ask them whether they want it or not. Am I not in a way manipulating others and myself by doing this practice, practising only in order to feel good myself?

**Rinpoche:** We can begin developing our own compassion by thinking of somebody we love very much and then trying to increase what we feel and extend it to other people. But when we visualise Chenrezig's light touching all sentient beings, we're not developing our own compassion but trying to benefit these beings. If we want to benefit them, to have them receive whatever is best for them, we don't need to have their prior consent. There's no need to ask them whether we may help them or not! Don't we all want to be happy? Our only problem is that we don't know how to achieve that objective.

It's true that some people refuse help, even if they know that the advice they receive would be good for them. We can tell a friend that it would be good for him to drink less – and he may know it himself – but he may not listen to us and may carry on drinking too much. If we can 'manipulate' him in such a way that he stops drinking, I don't think we can be reproached for that.

**Q:** I'm not sure.

**Rinpoche:** I'm completely sure! We're not binding his hands or putting him in prison. If somehow, through our inspiration, through whatever we say or do, we cure that person from his drinking problem, that's very good for him. I think there's nothing wrong with trying to help other beings as much as possible, even without their permission. They actually all want to be helped. We don't want to give people anything they don't want; we only want to give them what they want. So where's the problem?

The first aspect of this meditation is that you're working on yourself. You're trying to generate or activate the compassion and wisdom of all the Buddhas to help all sentient beings. You can call it a 'manipulation' if you wish. Whether it actually helps them or not depends on many things, but at least you're trying to help. Nothing ever happens just because of one isolated cause. Everything happens because of a combination of many factors. If you practise well enough, and if the circumstances are right, it may really help other beings; but sometimes, however much good energy you send, it may not work. It's not just your sending, there are many other factors involved too. However, it works at least on yourself more strongly than on other people because your mind is concentrated in a positive way. When you visualise Chenrezig, you can't possibly have negative thoughts at the same time, can you? Chenrezig is your own projection of all you think of as positive, so you cannot feel negative when you concentrate on his image. You're making your mind concentrate on what is positive – you can call it 'manipulating' if you like, and you're also receiving love, compassion and all the positive energies from Chenrezig. You're therefore strongly developing this positive side and thinking positively and beneficially towards all sentient beings. Of course, you cannot see the face of each and every sentient being. You don't even know them or how many they are, and that doesn't matter: you're sending this good energy to benefit, liberate and heal them all. You are feeling that; whether they feel it or not is not the main aspect here. If they feel and receive it, it's good, but if they don't, it doesn't matter. But you are feeling, you are developing a positive and beneficial mental attitude towards all sentient beings. This practice works therefore at many different levels on you, and that is the main result.

As to developing faith in the practice, it's a different matter. According to the Buddhist point of view, faith comes from understanding. Therefore, the more you understand what you're doing, the more your faith will grow because faith is based on experience.

**Q:** Am I not just substituting a positive concept for a negative one? Shouldn't we get rid of all concepts instead of just substituting one for another?

**RINPOCHE:** It's definitely better to substitute something positive for something negative. Very much better. We aren't talking here about concepts. These feelings may be concepts also, in a way, but what we are trying to do here is to replace negative emotions, feelings and thoughts by positive emotions, feelings and thoughts. These are not just concepts; they are your feeling, your experience. That's very important.

When we talk about 'being free of all concepts', we're actually talking about the ultimate level, the ultimate realisation. It's also connected to the practice we are explaining, as non-conceptual meditation also appears at some point, namely when we come to the 'completion stage'. However, 'non-conceptual' doesn't mean that we don't think at all, that we don't know anything and that our mind just remains blank. That has nothing to do with 'non-conceptual' or with getting rid of concepts. Instead of becoming 'blank', our mind has a very clear and direct understanding of its own nature. It's no longer just an intellectual understanding but a real experience of the way things are.

**Q:** For what exact reason are we so attached to the perceptions of the five senses?

**RINPOCHE:** It's probably because they're the only things we can experience. For the moment, we don't have the capacity to feel the peace and bliss of our natural inner mind. The only contacts or sensations that we can experience happen through our five senses, so our five senses overpower us. We're totally dependent on them and are constantly getting caught in assessments of what's nice, what's not nice, what's kind of neither. We get attached to these experiences of the five senses. Attachment is not only grasping at good things but also at bad things, at what is not pleasant. We strongly reject what we consider unpleasant. Aversion and attachment are two forms of this grasping process, they generate tremendous suffering. We live in constant fear as we crave the good sensations and try to avoid the uncomfortable ones, and all the other sufferings and problems come up. So that's the main reason.

As long as we react in this way, under the power of the five senses, we can't be peaceful and free. We therefore have to find a way to free ourselves from this dependence. When we can rely more on our inner strength or inner experience, then we can work on our sensations of pleasure and displeasure and lessen our attachment and aversion to things. We can let them pass by.

It is definitely possible to free ourselves from fear and anxiety. That's the reason why we meditate. We strengthen our inner mental consciousness. When the inner consciousness is more powerful, we're no longer under the power of the five senses. The five senses function normally but they no longer control us.

**Q:** When I do purification practices, I can't help having doubts creeping in and thinking that this is too easy, that one can't so easily get rid of all one's negative actions and tendencies. Another problem for me is that, in the beginning, I was taking the commitment not to do such bad things again with a lot of enthusiasm. OK, now, I'll never do that again. But then I would see myself doing it again and again, over and over. How can I promise every day not to make such mistakes again when I see myself keeping on doing it all the time? So I feel I can't really purify myself. And how can I invite all other sentient beings to share my visualisation? I don't feel pure enough. Whatever I send to them is mixed with my impure energy and I wonder whether I'm not actually harming them.

**RINPOCHE:** When trying to purify the negative parts of ourselves, the first thing, I think, is to become aware of this negative aspect. 'Negative' means, as you know, something that is bringing or causing sufferings and problems for us and others. Understanding clearly that we don't want to bring sufferings and problems to ourselves and others, we naturally wish to stop doing those actions that bring such problems and we feel regret about having done such things, knowingly or unknowingly. That is not difficult, is it? Now at least we're aware of the harmful aspect of negative actions. To know they're not useful, not beneficial for anybody, is the starting point of the purification.

How well you'll be able to abstain from doing negative things depends on many factors. First, since you're not – at least at the moment – a complete Buddha, you haven't completely eliminated your negative emotions and therefore it's not realistic to expect that you won't make any more mistakes. So it's OK in a way – I mean, it's not OK, but that's your situation. At least you regret whatever negative things you've done, especially those you cling to, like deep-rooted hatred and things you can't forgive, and you wish you could let them go. You no longer want to keep them.

This deep wish to be able to let them go is the second important step. Of course your negative emotions and tendencies won't go away after having recited the OM MANI PADME HUNG mantra for thirty minutes. That's normal. These negative tendencies are deeply rooted; they have built up over a long period, over many lifetimes, and we can't expect to get rid of them easily and quickly. We have to work on it constantly with courage and perseverance.

As to your negative energies, you shouldn't worry too much. When you take the bodhisattva vows, you say that you wish to bring all the sentient beings to enlightenment. This shows a strong courage, a strong motivation. This is why sometimes, when we rejoice at the thought of our bodhisattva attitude, we say that we have actually invited all sentient beings to Buddhahood. However, although we say that, the beings themselves don't know that we're thinking about them. So you haven't given them any trouble by meditating on them. You're trying to send them your benevolent thoughts, energy and compassion, but they don't know that you're doing it, so you're not giving them any hardship. You haven't sent them invitations asking them to come from all over the world to the place where you meditate. So I think there's no problem in thinking about all sentient beings and trying to send them your positive, healing energy. You do it from your own side, and although you can't do in a completely pure way because you're not completely pure, it doesn't mean that you're contaminating them with impure energy.

We send negative things when we are negative, whether we consciously send them or not. If, for instance, you're angry and upset with me, that vibration will be felt by everybody else here, won't it? In the same way, when you develop a positive, generous state of mind, it radiates, it has its own energy and you can send it to others. How strong it is depends on many things. We try to generate as much positive energy, compassion and wisdom as possible, but we are not alone. It's not only our own 'production' that we try to send, but we also try, in a way, to channel the energy, the blessings, the wisdom and compassion of all the enlightened beings.

We try to send it to every being but actually we're the ones receiving it most strongly. We can't possibly concentrate on such positive aspects and simultaneously be negative. Therefore this practice mainly works on our own mind.

**Q:** What are the necessary preconditions for Vajrayana practices? For the last two years, I've been hearing two contradictory positions concerning this. The first position is that one just needs to take refuge before one enters into Vajrayana practice, be it Tara or the ngondro or whatever, and then everything else will come naturally on the way. The other position is that it needs several years of Hinayana or Mahayana practice, for instance shinay practice or Lam Rim and Lojong, and that one needs to work on the basics before entering into Vajrayana practice, which is the highest practice. I'm a little confused about this.

**RINPOCHE:** We have these three vehicles or yanas: the Hinayana – or I would rather prefer Shravakayana because 'Hinayana' is a little disparaging; 'Hina' means small, so it means small yana, which is not a very good term – the Mahayana and the Vajrayana, and you should understand their relationships as follows.

The Shravakayana encompasses the basic teachings of the Buddha that are common to all three yanas. The Mahayana teachings are not included in the Shravakayana but they are included in the Vajrayana. The Mahayana is regarded as a part of the Vajrayana. We cannot practice the Vajrayana without the Mahayana teachings, which are its basis. So the Vajrayana actually includes all three.

We could represent it graphically as three concentric circles. The first small circle at the centre represents the Shravakayana teachings. The bigger circle is the Mahayana, and the biggest one, encompassing the other two, is the Vajrayana. This means that, if one practises Vajrayana, one automatically practises the other yanas as well, because they are part of it. We could say that the Vajrayana is the most 'inclusive' tradition. We cannot practise Vajrayana if we exclude the two other yanas.

If you understand that, you can say that you practise Vajrayana even as a beginner, because Vajrayana is not restricted to the specific 'Vajrayana practices' only; Vajrayana encompasses all the teachings. You can practise whatever is the best for you at this moment, whatever you understand, or whatever you can do, and still consider that you practise Vajrayana. Within Vajrayana, you can practise everything else.

For one who engages on the path of Vajrayana, there is no one and only way. This is of course true for all Buddhist teachings. There's no one right way. You can't say that someone can't practise this without having done that before; that one must first do so many years of Lojong and Lam Rim before being allowed to do some other practice. It varies from person to person. It depends on the interests of the person, on the circumstances, on the teachings one has received, on so many different conditions. Of course, one can establish a kind of curriculum, a graded course that will lead the student slowly from one level to the next. Within this context, a student can be advised to study something first before studying something else. This approach will help him or her understand progressively, more deeply, and have a stable foundation. That is also possible. But this doesn't mean that it's impossible for somebody to practise Vajrayana from the start without having stepped through the preliminaries.

The Vajrayana practice is very deep, of course. But one can't say that a beginner can't practise it. It depends on many things, mainly on the person's trust and connections. Some people feel naturally attracted towards a certain practice and they have a very good feeling when doing it. In such case, that practice is good for them, even if it's not the simplest practice and would maybe not be the first thing to start with when following a gradual approach. Maybe that person has more connections with it – for instance he or she may have practised it in a former life. We can't generalise about anything or say that there's only one possible approach. It also depends on how much you yourself understand your practice. If you do a certain practice and you're comfortable with it, you get something out of it, that's a good practice for you.

Some people have the idea that Vajrayana practice is more difficult. It's not true; Vajrayana practice is not more difficult. If one knows how to practise, it may even be easier in a way, because one can rely on many different techniques and methods that are put together to work on different aspects. In the Sutrayana approach we only apply one method at a time, whereas in the Vajrayana approach many different things happen at the same time. That's why it is said that Vajrayana has more means, more methods, which is actually the main difference between Vajrayana and the other yanas. When we practise Vajrayana, we do exactly the same thing as in the other yanas. The objectives remain identical. Whether we practice the Shravakayana, Mahayana or Vajrayana, we are only working on our mind, our emotions, our perceptions, our attitude. It's all about working on the mind, whatever yana we follow. Only the methods vary. Sometimes we use only one method at a time, sometimes we use a few methods at one time, sometimes we use many. This is mainly where the difference lies.

You don't have to be afraid of the Vajrayana. Of course, it's sometimes said that practising Vajrayana is like putting a snake in a tube: the snake can only crawl upward and come out from the top or crawl down and come out from the bottom; there's no way for him to get out somewhere in between. This can sound dangerous, and frighten people. However, I think there is no danger unless we use it in a very bad way. Vajrayana practice is not that dangerous. The basic point in all the practices is to have a good heart. Whatever we do, if we do it with a good heart, then it's good and our practice will be fruitful. Even saying one mantra is useful if we say it with a good intention and a good heart.

**Q:** I'm working with physically and mentally disabled people, some of whom have been kept in psychiatric institutions and clinics for twenty or thirty years. They're very dependent and can't take care of themselves. My job is to help them learn how to develop more autonomy. I encounter a lot of resistance from them because they are used to being cared for. They're scared of being independent in a way. Some of them aren't even able to speak. Sometimes, the only way I can teach them simple things, like eating with a spoon, or going to the toilet alone – things they'd normally be able to do but seem to have forgotten – is to force them. I sometimes wonder whether this is the bodhisattva way?

**Rinpoche:** I think it is very good to teach them how to do that. Of course, it's hard to teach anybody anything. It's a hard job to teach all of you too! It's the same thing. We talk about practices like Hinayana, Mahayana, Vajrayana, but there's no shortcut, no 'one thing' that we can do that would solve all problems at once. We have to work and work and work. It may not sound very exciting, but it's interesting. To change a habit is not easy; it's very difficult. Therefore we need patience, perseverance, courage and inspiration. Then only may we hope to change our usual way of reacting a little bit.

If you try to help these people with a good intention, it's very good. You can call it 'bodhisattva' work or whatever – what you call it doesn't matter – but it's very positive. It's not easy to make people learn things, especially mentally impaired persons. You have to be very patient, and try again and again. Of course, you can't be too harsh or you'll encounter a stronger resistance. This is a normal reaction. If somebody gives you orders – "You must do this! You must do that!" - your first thought will be, "How can I escape it? How can I get out of this?" So you should persevere but try to keep your approach as smooth as possible, and remain very patient, and if there is only very little result, don't blame yourself. Don't feel too bad if you can't make people learn what you would like them to. It's sometimes very frustrating even to teach people without any particular disability. To teach disabled people is of course much more difficult, so there's no need for you to feel frustrated.

**Q:** When I try to develop love and compassion, sometimes feelings of aggression and anger come up. I'm trying to handle these emotions by trying to relax within them but it proves almost impossible. I feel as if my head and body were separate from each other. There's a great tension in the head, as if everything was pushing on it. I don't know why I feel this anger. It's not directed at anyone in particular; it spreads out to everything around me. It's not an aggression that I can pinpoint; it's almost as if the aggression was spreading from everywhere. I really do have the wish to develop love and compassion but this feeling of aggression overwhelms me. I then have to relax and calm down and start again and concentrate on love and compassion. Is there anything I can do?

**RINPOCHE:** Why not 'enjoy' this aggressiveness? Yes! You acknowledge the presence of these emotions. There they are. It's OK. Sometimes, such emotions come up. Where's the problem? It will dissolve if you don't fight it. You don't need to feel so much aversion towards these aggressive feelings. When they manifest, you can even use them in a tonglen practice. You can pray that all the aggressive and angry feelings in the whole world be absorbed in your own feeling of aggression and that all beings may thus be liberated from such feelings. You can pray that you may be the only one to experience such feelings and that, thanks to your practice, all beings may enjoy perfect peace and happiness. And then you can have a nice 'aggression session'!

You will then discover a particular rule or law, namely that what you want to stay for a long time never stays for long time! The aggression will dissolve on its own.

**Q:** Is there anything else we can do for people who have died quite a long time ago and regarding whom we have quite foreboding feelings, in the sense that we aren't too sure whether they took rebirth in a good place and we rather fear that the place they're now might be pretty bad? Can we actually do something for those people or is it just an illusion to think that we can help them by our practice?

**RINPOCHE:** From a Buddhist point of view, if one does something positive, there's a positive result and if one does something negative, there's a negative result.

If we do something positive and then dedicate the beneficial results for a particular purpose, there's a certain power, a certain strength attached to it. It's therefore possible – although maybe not necessarily always the case – that there is some benefit to the person for whom we are dedicating our practice. However it's generally believed that it has a stronger, more powerful effect on ourselves. In this way, if we try to help somebody else through practices, positive actions or whatever, it actually helps both of us to some degree.

Whether somebody is alive, has just died or has been dead for a long time doesn't make much difference. When we try to help someone through practice, prayers and meditation, how much help the beneficiary receives depends on many things. The prayer or the practice in itself is not the only element to consider. It also depends on our own level of spiritual development. If our mind is clear and calm, if we're very concentrated, if we have a high level of spiritual development, the effect of our practice will be much stronger. It also partly depends on the receptivity of the person for whom we are practising. The effectiveness of one and the same practice can thus vary greatly according to the circumstances.

It is also supposed to help in different subtle ways that are difficult to assess through our ordinary perceptions. Although not clearly or immediately visible, the effect may be there at a deeper level. There's a Milarepa story that illustrates this well.

Milarepa once went to a high snowy mountain to meditate. While he was up in his cave, snow started to fall heavily. It snowed for weeks and the path to the cave was completely blocked for the whole winter. Milarepa didn't have provisions for five or six months and his students were sadly convinced that their teacher had died, that there was no hope of seeing him again. They organised a ceremony for his death with prayers, tsog pujas, and other rituals. When spring came and the snow began to melt and the path was again accessible, the students went to the cave to get their master's dead body. They found Milarepa in the cave, but to their great surprise and delight, he was alive and even quite healthy. Milarepa told them that, on certain days, he had had the impression of eating a large and nourishing meal and had felt very comfortable.

These had been precisely the days when the students had organised the tsog pujas for him. Milarepa laughed and remarked that in this case, maybe tsog pujas were quite a good thing to do, because he had really felt as if he had eaten a lot.

Recently, researches have been conducted on the effectiveness of prayer. The researchers came to the conclusion that praying sometimes produces effects, and that the prayer's efficacy has nothing to do with distance. Whether the person for whom one prays is nearby or far away doesn't make any difference. Time is no problem either, because even if somebody died long ago, he or she is still somewhere. If neither time nor distance is an obstacle, then we can definitely pray and practise in order to benefit people who've died many years ago. We should try to do something positive, any positive action we can think of, and then dedicate its positive result for the benefit of all beings in general and that person in particular.

From a Buddhist point of view, a positive deed is something you do inspired by loving kindness, compassion, the wish to help others. Conversely, a negative deed is an action that is motivated by negative emotions. Anything that you do with anger, jealousy, pride or attachment is a negative deed. For instance, if you do something with good intentions that is concretely helping others, such as charity work, that's very good. Something that doesn't help in a material way but which you do with the intention of benefiting others, like a spiritual practice, prayers or meditation, should also be regarded as a positive deed. Even studying can be considered a positive deed if inspired by a positive motivation. Almost anything can be a positive deed if your motivation is really good, so what you do is entirely up to you. There's nothing like a list of the positive deeds you should do!

**Q:** Could you please explain the background and purpose of tsog pujas? I can't relate to the explanations I've heard so far. I was told that the participants in a tsog puja visualise themselves as deities and that the offerings contain meat and sometimes alcohol. I heard that the function of such rituals is to change impure things into pure things.

**RINPOCHE:** The Sanskrit term is ganachakra, which has been translated as 'tsog khor' in Tibetan. 'Tsog' means gathering, and 'khor' is a wheel; so it's the wheel of gatherings.

In the beginning, when Vajrayana was practised secretly, practitioners would come together and have a meal that was at the same time a practice. The 'tsog khor' probably comes from that tradition. It can accompany any tantric practice that belongs to tantras higher than Yoga Tantra.

The meal, the festive part of the tsog (a tsog has many different parts), is a way of working on our five senses. The method may be different, but the objective is the same as in all the other Buddhist practices. It's based on the understanding of the emptiness and fundamental sameness of everything. With this understanding as background, the tsog is a practical way of taking things as they come, of not distinguishing too much between good and bad, pure and impure. Through the tsog practice, we're trying to work on our strong aversion to bad, unclean things, and on our attachment to what is beautiful, nice, pure and attractive. This is why we find meat and alcohol in a tsog practice. Whatever has been brought by the participants is shared between them all and they are supposed to eat anything, whatever is there, whatever is available. It's an exercise in getting rid of concepts, of rigid ideas of good and bad.

This training very much belongs to a Vajrayana level of practice and it can be misunderstood by people who practise at the level of the Shravakayana or Mahayana. We should understand that we have three levels of precepts: the Vinaya, the Bodhisattvayana and the Vajrayana precepts.

The Vinaya strictly states what is right and wrong, good and bad, what one can and cannot do. The Bodhisattvayana precepts are a little less clear-cut, as the motivation behind an action comes into consideration. A particular action isn't always bad or good in itself; its value depends on the particular situation and the intention that motivates it. The Vajrayana goes still further. It aims at complete freedom and, at some stage, you should liberate yourself from even good things that still bind you.

This is actually why the Vajrayana was kept so secret: because this approach can be misused by people who don't have the right understanding. It can be dangerous to say to somebody who isn't ready, who hasn't reached a high level of spiritual development, that everything that's binding him is wrong, even the sacred precepts he vowed to respect. That's why Vajrayana was kept so secret.

The tsog is a big and not very easy subject in itself. To do it properly is quite deep and complicated. At a simple level, it's also an offering to our teacher and all our vajra brothers and sisters, and enjoying ourselves while perceiving everything purely. We visualise ourselves and the people around us as deities, which means that we develop confidence in our true nature, in our pure essence. Within that pure perception, whatever actions we perform are divine actions and whatever we eat is a pure substance of 'one taste'.

Eating becomes an offering because our body is the mandala of the hundred wrathful and peaceful deities. From a Vajrayana point of view a human being is an aggregate of all the deities. It's not an impure but a pure aggregate, which is why, in the Vajrayana, our body is always regarded as a mandala. The cosmos outside is the outer mandala, the body inside is the inner mandala, and the mind is also a mandala. Perceiving these three levels of mandalas corresponds to having the pure vision: we have no ego but the pure vision of the mandala inside, outside, everywhere. Within this state, we're completely free from fear, free from attachment, free from aversion. There's nothing but the completely pure nature of everything. There's nothing but the deities and pure mandalas. This state is the enlightened state. This is what the tsog puja is somehow related to.

**Q:** What does the swastika stand for in Buddhism? As you know, for us it's associated with Nazism and the Third Reich, but what's the original meaning of this sign?

**RINPOCHE:** The swastika is a very old Indian symbol. 'Swasti' means good luck, everything good. It's a symbol of stability. In Tibet, this symbol was mostly used by Bönpos; Buddhists didn't use it very much.

I think Hitler chose this sign because it comes from India, to point to the Indian origin of the Aryan race. There's nothing wrong with the symbol itself. The sign is much older than Hitler.

In India, you'll find many images bearing the swastika. Some look like Buddha images but most of the time they're not the Buddha but a contemporary of the Buddha, Jain Mahavira, the founder of the Jain religion. He's represented like the

Buddha and sometimes the only detail that differentiates him from the Buddha is the presence of this swastika symbol.

**Q:** Could you please bless the text of my practice?

**Rinpoche:** What we call 'rabnay' is the blessing of images and inanimate objects. It's similar to the empowerment given to people. Through this blessing, we try to bring the wisdom energy into that particular object.

However, books never need any blessing. Books are already blessed because they're the Buddha's words; they are the Dharma. When one reads a Dharma text, one actually gets the blessing from it. That's why there's a Tibetan saying, 'Don't place even a Buddha image on top of the Buddha scriptures'. This means that images are not more but less important than texts. The scriptures contain the understanding, the meaning – everything – and therefore we Tibetans show great respect towards the texts. We never step over a book or place shoes on a text. It's sometimes said that one shouldn't disregard even one letter, like a letter 'na', because even such a small letter represents the Dharma. This attitude may seem a little extreme but you should understand it comes from the fact that in the past, in Tibet, writing was mainly used to reproduce scriptures and teachings.

**Q:** May I wash a protection cord? Is this some kind of everlasting protection?

**Rinpoche:** When we bless something, we pray that all the Buddhas of the three times and the ten directions may come and reside in this object and bless all sentient beings until the object itself is destroyed or disintegrates into its five constituting elements. The blessing is thus supposed to be effective until the object is worn out and falls apart.

I think there's nothing wrong with washing a protection cord. You don't need to wash it too often or keep it too clean either. Recently, I gave a nice gilded statue to one of my students. She cleaned and brushed it so much that all the gold was rubbed off!

As a last remark, if you have to dispose of a blessed object, try to do it in a nice way if possible. It's better to burn it rather than to throw it away in the dustbin.

**Q:** My bad habits always lead me into the wrong direction. What can I do if all of a sudden I realise that I am going in the wrong direction? How can I get back? Could you give me a kind of 'hook' or some good advice I could use to keep to the right path?

**RINPOCHE:** The moment you understand that you're going in the wrong direction, just stop and turn back. Think of when you miss the right turning on the road. You do the same thing. If you're driving from Hamburg to Halscheid, and you realise you've missed the turning, then, as soon as you find this out, you try to get back on the right road, don't you? That's all!

*All my babbling,*
*In the name of Dharma*
*Has been set down faithfully*
*By my dear students of pure vision.*

*I pray that at least a fraction of the wisdom*
*Of those enlightened teachers*
*Who tirelessly trained me*
*Shines through this mass of incoherence.*

*May the sincere efforts of all those*
*Who have worked tirelessly*
*Result in spreading the true meaning of Dharma*
*To all who aspire to know.*

*May this also help to dispel the darkness of ignorance*
*In the minds of all living beings*
*And lead them to complete realisation*
*Free from all fear.*

*Ringu Tulku 1997*

ཕྱགས་རྗེ་ཆེན་པོའི་བསྒོམ་བཟླས་འགྲོ་དོན་མཁའ་ཁྱབ་མ་བཞུགས་སོ།

# All-Pervading Benefit of Beings

## The Meditation and Recitation of the Great Compassionate One

*The refuge and bodhichitta for the meditation and recitation of the Great Compassionate One:*

SANG GYE CHÖ DANG TSHOK KYI CHOK NAM LA
In the supreme Buddha, dharma and assembly,

CHANG CHUB BAR DU DAK NI KYAP SU CHI
I take refuge until attaining enlightenment.

DAK GI JIN SOK GYI PE SÖ NAM KYI
Through the merit of practicing generosity and so on,

DRO LA PHEN CHIR SANG GYE DRUP PAR SHOK
May I attain Buddhahood in order to benefit beings.

*Repeat three times.*

*Visualizing the deity:*

DAK SOK KHA KHYAB SEM CEN GYI
On the crown of the head of myself and others —
sentient beings pervading space,

CI TSUK PE KAR DA WE TENG
On a white lotus and moon, is HRI.

HRI LE PHAK CHOK CEN RE ZI
From it appears noble and supreme Avalokita.

KAR SAL Ö ZER NGA DEN THRO
He is brilliant white and radiates the five lights.

མཛེས་འཛུམ་ཐུགས་རྗེའི་སྤྱན་གྱིས་གཟིགས།

DZE DZUM THUK JEY CEN GYI ZIK

Handsome and smiling, he looks on with eyes of compassion.

ཕྱག་བཞིའི་དང་པོ་ཐལ་སྦྱར་མཛད།

CHAK ZHI DANG PO THAL JAR DZE

He has four hands: the first are joined in añjali,

འོག་གཉིས་ཤེལ་ཕྲེང་པད་དཀར་བསྣམས།

OK NYI SHEL THRENG PE KAR NAM

The lower two hold a crystal māla and a white lotus.

དར་དང་རིན་ཆེན་རྒྱན་གྱིས་སྤྲས།

DAR DANG RIN CHEN GYEN GYI TRE

Adorned with ornaments of silks and jewels,

རི་དྭགས་པགས་པས་སྟོད་གཡོགས་གསོལ།

RI DAK PAK PE TÖ YOK SÖL

He wears an upper garment of deerskin.

ཨོད་དཔག་མེད་པའི་དབུ་རྒྱན་ཅན།

ÖPAK ME PE U GYEN CEN
Amitābha crowns his head.

ཞབས་གཉིས་རྡོ་རྗེ་སྐྱིལ་ཀྲུང་བཞུགས།

ZHAP NYI DORJE KYIL TRUNG ZHUK
His two feet are in the vajra posture.

དྲི་མེད་ཟླ་བར་རྒྱབ་བརྟེན་པ།

DRI ME DA WAR GYAP TEN PA
His back rests against a stainless moon.

སྐྱབས་གནས་ཀུན་འདུས་ངོ་བོར་འགྱུར།

KYAP NE KÜN DÜ NGO WOR GYUR
He is the embodiment of all objects of refuge.

*All-Pervading Benefit of Beings*

*Think that you and all sentient beings are supplicating with one voice:*

JO WO KYÖN GYI MA GÖ KU DOK KAR
Lord, white in color, unstained by faults,

DZOK SANG GYE KYI U LA GYEN
A perfect Buddha adorning your head,

THUK JEY CEN GYI DRO LA ZIK
You look upon beings with eyes of compassion.

CEN RE ZI LA CHAK TSHAL LO
Avalokita, we prostrate to you.

*Recite that as many times as you can.*

ཡན་ལག་བདུན་པ་ནི།

*The seven-branch prayer:*

འཕགས་མཆོག་སྤྱན་རས་གཟིགས་དབང་དང་།
PHAK CHOK CEN RE ZI WANG DANG
To noble lord Avalokita

ཕྱོགས་བཅུ་དུས་གསུམ་བཞུགས་པ་ཡི།
CHOK CU DÜ SUM ZHUK PA YI
And to all the Buddhas and their heirs

རྒྱལ་བ་སྲས་བཅས་ཐམས་ཅད་ལ།
GYAL WA SE CE THAM CE LA
Of the ten directions and three times,

ཀུན་ནས་དང་བས་ཕྱག་འཚལ་ལོ།
KÜN NE DANG WE CHAK TSHAL LO
We prostrate with joyful faith.

ME TOK DUK PÖ MAR ME DRI
We make offerings, those actual and those emanated by mind:

ZHAL ZE RÖL MO LA SOK PA
Flowers, incense, light, perfume,

NGÖ JOR YI KYI TRÜL NE PHÜL
Food, music, and so on.

PHAK PE TSHOK KYI ZHE SU SOL
Assembly of noble ones, please accept them.

ཐོག་མ་མེད་ནས་ད་ལྟའི་བར།

THOK MA ME NE DA TE BAR
From beginningless time until now,

མི་དགེ་བཅུ་དང་མཚམས་མེད་ལྔ།

MI GE CU DANG TSHAM ME NGA
Our minds overpowered by mental afflictions,

སེམས་ནི་ཉོན་མོངས་དབང་གྱུར་པའི།

SEM NI NYÖN MONG WANG GYUR PE
We have committed the ten nonvirtuous actions and the five acts of immediate consequence.

སྡིག་པ་ཐམས་ཅད་བཤགས་པར་བགྱི།

DIK PA THAM CE SHAK PAR GYI
We confess all these negative actions.

*All-Pervading Benefit of Beings*

NYEN THÖ RANG GYAL CHANG CHUB SEM
We rejoice in the merit

SO SÖ KYE WO LA SOK PE
Of whatever virtue has been accumulated

DÜ SUM GE WA CI SAK PE
By hearers, solitary realizers, bodhisattvas,

SÖ NAM LA NI DAK YI RANG
And ordinary beings throughout the three times.

སེམས་ཅན་རྣམས་ཀྱི་བསམ་པ་དང་།

SEM CEN NAM KYI SAM PA DANG
In accordance with the diverse capabilities

བློ་ཡི་བྱེ་བྲག་ཇི་ལྟ་བར།

LO YI JE DRAK JI TA WAR
And aspirations of sentient beings,

ཆེ་ཆུང་ཐུན་མོང་ཐེག་པ་ཡི།

CHE CHUNG THUN MONG THEK PA YI
We request you to turn the wheel of dharma

ཆོས་ཀྱི་འཁོར་ལོ་བསྐོར་དུ་གསོལ།

CHÖ KYI KHOR LO KOR DU SÖL
Of the greater, lesser, or conventional vehicles.

འཁོར་བ་ཇི་སྲིད་མ་སྟོངས་བར།

KHOR WA JI MA TONG BAR
Not passing into nirvāna

མྱ་ངན་མི་འདའ་ཐུགས་རྗེ་ཡིས།

NYA NGEN MI DA THUK JE YI
Until samsāra is emptied,

སྡུག་བསྔལ་རྒྱ་མཚོར་བྱིང་བ་ཡི།

DUK NGEL GYAM TSHOR JING WA YI
Please look with compassion on sentient beings

སེམས་ཅན་རྣམས་ལ་གཟིགས་སུ་གསོལ།

SEM CAN NAM LA ZIK SU SÖL
Drowning in the ocean of suffering.

བདག་གིས་བསོད་ནམས་ཅི་བསགས་པ།

DAK GI SÖ NAM CI SAK PA
May all the merit we have accumulated

ཐམས་ཅད་བྱང་ཆུབ་རྒྱུར་གྱུར་ནས།

THAM CE CHANG CHUB GYUR GYUR NE
Become a cause for enlightenment.

རིང་པོར་མི་ཐོགས་འགྲོ་བ་ཡི།

RING POR MI THOK DRO WA YI
Without delay, may we become

འདྲེན་པའི་དཔལ་དུ་བདག་གྱུར་ཅིག །

DREN PE PAL DU DAK GYUR CIK
A glorious guide for beings.

*All-Pervading Benefit of Beings*

གདུང་འབོད་ཀྱི་གསོལ་འདེབས་ནི།

*The supplication of calling with longing:*

གསོལ་བ་འདེབས་སོ་བླ་མ་སྤྱན་རས་གཟིགས།

SÖL WA DEP SO LA MA CEN RE ZI

We supplicate you, guru Avalokita.

གསོལ་བ་འདེབས་སོ་ཡི་དམ་སྤྱན་རས་གཟིགས།

SÖL WA DEP SO YI DAM CEN RE ZI

We supplicate you, yidam Avalokita.

གསོལ་བ་འདེབས་སོ་འཕགས་མཆོག་སྤྱན་རས་གཟིགས།

SÖL WA DEP SO PHAK CHOK CEN RE ZI

We supplicate you, supreme noble Avalokita.

གསོལ་བ་འདེབས་སོ་སྐྱབས་མགོན་སྤྱན་རས་གཟིགས།

SÖL WA DEP SO KYAP GÖN CEN RE ZI

We supplicate you, lord of refuge Avalokita.

གསོལ་བ་འདེབས་སོ་བྱམས་མགོན་སྤྱན་རས་གཟིགས།

SÖL WA DEP SO CHAM GÖN CEN RE ZI

We supplicate you, loving protector Avalokita.

ཐུགས་རྗེས་ཟུངས་ཤིག་རྒྱལ་བ་ཐུགས་རྗེ་ཅན།

THUK JE ZUNG SHIK GYAL WA THUK JE CEN

Embrace us with your compassion, compassionate victorious one.

*All-Pervading Benefit of Beings*

མཐའ་མེད་འཁོར་བར་གྲངས་མེད་འཁྱམས་གྱུར་ཅིང་།

THA ME KHOR WAR DRANG ME KHYAM GYUR CING

For beings who have wandered through countless aeons in endless samsāra

བཟོད་མེད་སྡུག་བསྔལ་མྱོང་བའི་འགྲོ་བ་ལ།

ZÖ ME DUK NGEL NYONG WE DRO WA LA

And experience unbearable suffering,

མགོན་པོ་ཁྱེད་ལས་སྐྱབས་གཞན་མ་མཆིས་སོ།

GÖN PO KHYE LE KYAP ZHEN MA CHI SO

There is no other refuge but you, lord.

རྣམ་མཁྱེན་སངས་རྒྱས་ཐོབ་པར་བྱིན་གྱིས་རློབས།

NAM KHYEN SANG GYE THOP PAR JIN GYI LOP

Grant your blessing that they may achieve omniscient Buddhahood.

ཐོག་མེད་དུས་ནས་ལས་ངན་བསགས་པའི་མཐུས།

THOK ME DÜ NE LE NGEN SAK PE THÜ
Because of accumulating negative karma from beginningless time,

ཞེ་སྡང་དབང་གིས་དམྱལ་བར་སྐྱེས་གྱུར་ཏེ།

ZHE DANG WANG GI NYAL WAR KYE GYUR TE
Due to aggression, sentient beings are born in the hells

ཚ་གྲང་སྡུག་བསྔལ་མྱོང་བའི་སེམས་ཅན་རྣམས།

TSHA DRANG DUK NGEL NYONG WE SEM CEN NAM
And experience the sufferings of hot and cold.

ལྷ་མཆོག་ཁྱེད་ཀྱི་དྲུང་དུ་སྐྱེ་བར་ཤོག །

LHA CHOK KHYE KYI DRUNG DU KYE WAR SHOK
May they be born in your presence, supreme deity.

ཨོཾ་མ་ཎི་པདྨེ་ཧཱུྃ།

OM MANI PADME HUNG

ཐོག་མེད་དུས་ནས་ལས་ངན་བསགས་པའི་མཐུས།

THOK ME DÜ NE LE NGEN SAK PE THÜ

Because of accumulating negative karma from beginningless time,

སེར་སྣའི་དབང་གིས་ཡི་དྭགས་གནས་སུ་སྐྱེས།

SER NE WANG GI YI DAK NE SU KYE

Due to miserliness, sentient beings are born in the hungry ghost realm

བཀྲེས་སྐོམ་སྡུག་བསྔལ་མྱོང་བའི་སེམས་ཅན་རྣམས།

TRE KOM DUK NGEL NYONG WE SEM CEN NAM

And experience the sufferings of hunger and thirst.

ཞིང་མཆོག་པོ་ཏ་ལ་རུ་སྐྱེ་བར་ཤོག །

ZHING CHOK PO TA LA RU KYE WAR SHOK

May they be born in your supreme pure land of Potala.

ཨོཾ་མ་ཎི་པདྨེ་ཧཱུྃ།

OM MANI PADME HUNG

THOG ME DÜ NE LE NGEN SAK PE THÜ
Because of accumulating negative karma from beginningless time,

TI MUK WANG GI DÜ DROR KYE GYUR TE
Due to bewilderment, sentient beings are born as animals

LEN KUK DUG NGEL NYONG WE SEM CEN NAM
And experience the sufferings of stupidity and dullness.

GÖN PO KHYE KYI DRUNG DU KYE WAR SHOK
May they be born in your presence, protector.

OM MANI PADME HUNG

ཐོག་མེད་དུས་ནས་ལས་ངན་བསགས་པའི་མཐུས།

THOG ME DÜ NE LE NGEN SAK PE THÜ

Because of accumulating negative karma from beginningless time,

འདོད་ཆགས་དབང་གིས་མི་ཡི་གནས་སུ་སྐྱེས།

DÖ CHAK WANG GI MI YI NE SU KYE

Due to desire, sentient beings are born in the human realm

བྲེལ་ཕོངས་སྡུག་བསྔལ་མྱོང་བའི་སེམས་ཅན་རྣམས།

DREL PHONG DUK NGEL NYONG WE SEM CEN NAM

And experience the sufferings of constant toil and poverty.

ཞིང་མཆོག་བདེ་བ་ཅན་དུ་སྐྱེ་བར་ཤོག །

ZHING CHOK PO TA LA RU KYE WAR SHOK

May they be born in your pure land of Sukhāvati.

ཨོཾ་མ་ཎི་པདྨེ་ཧཱུྃ།

OM MANI PADME HUNG

ཐོག་མེད་དུས་ནས་ལས་ངན་བསགས་པའི་མཐུས།

THOK ME DUS NE LE NGEN SAK PE THÜ

Because of accumulating negative karma from beginningless time,

ཕྲག་དོག་དབང་གིས་ལྷ་མིན་གནས་སུ་སྐྱེས།

THRAK DOK WANG GI LHA MIN NE SU KYE

Due to jealousy, sentient beings are born in the realm of the jealous gods

འཐབ་རྩོད་སྡུག་བསྔལ་མྱོང་བའི་སེམས་ཅན་རྣམས།

THAP TSÖ DUK NGEL NYONG WE SEM CEN NAM

And experience the sufferings of constant fighting and quarreling.

པོ་ཏ་ལ་ཡི་ཞིང་དུ་སྐྱེ་བར་ཤོག

PO TA LA YI ZHING DU KYE WAR SHOK

May they be born in your pure land of Potala.

ༀ་མ་ཎི་པདྨེ་ཧཱུྃ།

OM MANI PADME HUNG

THOG ME NE LE NGEN SAK PE THÜ
Because of accumulating negative karma from beginningless time,

NGA GYAL WANG GI LHA YI NE SU KYE
Due to pride, sentient beings are born in the realm of the gods

PHO TUNG DUK NGEL NYONG WE SEM CEN NAM
And experience the sufferings of death and falling.

PO TA LA YI ZHING DU KYE WAR SHOK
May they be born in your land of Potala.

OM MANI PADME HUNG

བདག་ནི་སྐྱེ་ཞིང་སྐྱེ་བ་ཐམས་ཅད་དུ། 

DAK NI KYE ZHING KYE WA THAM CE DU

Birth after birth, through all our lives,

སྤྱན་རས་གཟིགས་དང་མཛད་པ་མཚུངས་པ་ཡིས། 

CEN RE ZI DANG DZE PA TSHUNG PA YI

May we liberate beings of the impure realms

མ་དག་ཞིང་གི་འགྲོ་རྣམས་སྒྲོལ་བ་དང་། 

MA DAK ZHING GI DRO NAM DRÖL WA DANG

By activity equal to yours, Avalokita,

གསུང་མཆོག་ཡིག་དྲུག་ཕྱོགས་བཅུར་རྒྱས་པར་ཤོག 

SUNG CHOK YIK DRUK CHOK CUR GYE PAR SHOK

And may the supreme speech of your six syllables pervade the ten directions.

*All-Pervading Benefit of Beings*

འཕགས་མཆོག་ཁྱེད་ལ་གསོལ་བ་བཏབ་པའི་མཐུས།

PHAK CHOK KHYE LA SÖL WA TAB PE THÜ

Noble and supreme one, by the power of supplicating you,

བདག་གི་གདུལ་བྱར་གྱུར་པའི་འགྲོ་བ་རྣམས།

DAK GI DÜL JAR GYUR PE DRO WA NAM

May beings to be tamed by us

ལས་འབྲས་ལྷུར་ལེན་དགེ་བའི་ལས་ལ་བརྩོན།

LE DRE LHUR LEN GE WE LE LA TSÖN

Practice karma and its result and apply themselves to virtuous actions.

འགྲོ་བའི་དོན་དུ་ཆོས་དང་ལྡན་པར་ཤོག

DRO WE DÖN DU CHÖ DANG DEN PAR SHOK

May they act in harmony with dharma for the benefit of beings.

དེ་ལྟར་རྩེ་གཅིག་གསོལ་བཏབ་པས། 
DE TAR TSE CIK SÖL TAP PE
Due to supplicating one-pointedly in that way,

འཕགས་པའི་སྐུ་ལས་འོད་ཟེར་འཕྲོ། 
PHAK PE KU LE Ö ZER THRO
Light rays stream forth from the body of the Noble One

མ་དག་ལས་སྣང་འཁྲུལ་ཤེས་སྦྱངས། 
MA DAK LE NANG THRÜL SHE JANG
And purify impure karmic appearances and mistaken consciousness.

ཕྱི་སྣོད་བདེ་བ་ཅན་གྱི་ཞིང་། 
CHI NÖ DE WA CEN GYI ZHING
The outer world becomes the pure land of Sukhāvati.

ནང་བཅུད་སྐྱེ་འགྲོའི་ལུས་ངག་སེམས། 
NANG CÜ KYE DRÖ LÜ NGAK SEM
The body, speech and mind of the inhabitants within

*All-Pervading Benefit of Beings*

### CEN RE ZI WANG KU SUNG THUK
Become the body, speech and mind of Avalokita.

### NANG DRAK RIK TONG YER ME GYUR
Appearances, sounds and awareness are inseparable from emptiness.

*While meditating on the meaning of that,*
*recite the mantra as much as you can:*

### OM MANI PADME HUNG

*At the end, without conceptualizing the three spheres,*
*rest evenly in your own nature.*

བདག་གཞན་ལུས་སྣང་འཕགས་པའི་སྐུ།

DAK ZHEN LÜ NANG PHAK PE KU

The physical appearance of myself and others is the body of the Noble One.

སྒྲ་གྲགས་ཡི་གེ་དྲུག་པའི་དབྱངས།

DRA DRAK YI GE DRUK PE YANG

Sounds are the melody of the six syllables.

དྲན་རྟོག་ཡེ་ཤེས་ཆེན་པོའི་ཀློང་།

DREN TOK YE SHE CHEN PÖ LONG

Thoughts are the expanse of great wisdom.

GE WA DI YI NYUR DU DAK
By this merit, may we quickly

CEN RE ZI WANG DRUP GYUR NE
Accomplish Avalokiteshvara

DRO WA CIG KYANG MA LÜ PA
And establish every being without exception

DE YI SA LA GÖ PAR SHOK
In that state.

དེ་ལྟར་སྒོམ་བཟླས་བགྱིས་པའི་བསོད་ནམས་ཀྱིས།

DE TAR GOM DE GYI PE SÖ NAM KYI

By the merit of meditating and reciting in this way,

བདག་དང་བདག་ལ་འབྲེལ་ཐོགས་འགྲོ་བ་ཀུན།

DAK DANG DAK LA DREL THOK DRO WA KÜN

May we and all beings with whom we are connected

མི་གཙང་ལུས་འདི་བོར་བར་གྱུར་མ་ཐག །

MI TSANG LÜ DI BOR WAR GYUR MA THAK

Be miraculously born in Sukhāvati

བདེ་བ་ཅན་དུ་རྫུས་ཏེ་སྐྱེ་བར་ཤོག །

DE WA CEN DU DZÜ TE KYE WAR SHOK

As soon as we have left behind this impure body.

སྐྱེས་མ་ཐག་ཏུ་ས་བཅུ་རབ་བགྲོད་ནས།

KYE MA THAK TU SA CU RAP DRÖ NE

As soon as we are born there, may we traverse the ten bhumis

*All-Pervading Benefit of Beings*

TRÜL PE CHOK CUR ZHEN DÖN JE PAR CHOK
And benefit others in the ten directions through our emanations.

GE WA DI YI KYE WO KUN
By this merit, may all beings

SÖ NAM YE SHE TSHOK DZOK NE
Perfect the two accumulations of merit and wisdom

SÖ NAM YE SHE LE JUNG WE
And achieve the two genuine kāyas

DAM PA KU NYI THOP PAR SHOK
Arising from merit and wisdom.

CHANG CHUB SEM CHOK RIN PO CHE
In whomever the precious bodhichitta

MA KYE PA NAM KYE GYUR CIG
Has not arisen, may it arise.

KYE PA NYAM PA ME PA DANG
In whomever it has arisen, may it not decline,

GONG NE GONG DU PHUL WAR SHOK
But increase further and further.

*Short Sukhāvati Aspiration:*

E MA HO

NGO TSHAR SANG GYE NANG WA THA YE DANG
Wondrous Buddha Amitābha,

YE SU JO WO THUK JE CHEN PO DANG
On your right, Lord of Great Compassion,

YÖN DU SEM PA THU CHEN THOP NAM LA
On your left, Bodhisattva Attainer of Great Power,

SANG GYE CHANG SEM PAK ME KHOR GYI KOR
Surrounded by your immeasurable retinue of Buddhas and bodhisattvas.

༄༅། བདེ་སྐྱིད་ངོ་མཚར་དཔག་ཏུ་མེད་པ་ཡི༔

DE KYI NGO TSHAR PAK TU ME PA YI
In this Buddhafield known as Sukhāvati

བདེ་བ་ཅན་ཞེས་བྱ་བའི་ཞིང་ཁམས་དེར༔

DE WA CEN ZHE JA WE ZHING KHAM DER
Of wondrous, boundless joy and happiness,

བདག་ནི་འདི་ནས་ཚེ་འཕོས་གྱུར་མ་ཐག༔

DAK NI DI NE TSHE PHÖ GYUR MA THAK
May we be born, as soon as we depart from this life,

སྐྱེ་བ་གཞན་གྱིས་བར་མ་ཆོད་པ་རུ༔

KYE WA ZHEN GYI BAR MA CHÖ PA RU
Not taking other births in between,

དེ་རུ་སྐྱེས་ནས་སྣང་མཐའི་ཞལ་མཐོང་ཤོག༔

DE RU KYE NE NANG THE ZHAL THONG SHOK
And see the face of Amitābha.

*All-Pervading Benefit of Beings*

དེ་སྐད་བདག་གིས་སྨོན་ལམ་བཏབ་པ་འདིཿ

DE KE DAK GI MÖN LAM TAP PA DI
May all the Buddhas and bodhisattvas of the ten directions

ཕྱོགས་བཅུའི་སངས་རྒྱས་བྱང་སེམས་ཐམས་ཅད་ཀྱིསཿ

CHOK CÜ SANG GYE CHANG SEM THAM CE KYI
Grant their blessings so that our aspiration

གེགས་མེད་འགྲུབ་པར་བྱིན་གྱིས་བརླབ་ཏུ་གསོལཿ

GEK ME DRUP PAR JIN GYI LAP TU SÖL
May be accomplished without obstruction.

ཏད་ཡཐཱཿ པཉྩེནྡྲི་ཡ་ཨ་ཝ་བོ་དྷ་ནི་ཡེ་སྭཱ་ཧཱཿ

TEYATHA PENTSENDRIYA AWABODANIYE SO HA
TAD YATHÀ PAŃCHANDRIYA AVABHODANĀYE SVÀHÀ

The root text was written by Shangpa siddha, Thangtong Gyalpo. The *Seven-Branch Prayer* and *Supplication of Calling with Longing* were written by Pema Karpo. The Abbreviated *Sukkāvāti Supplication* is a terma received by Mingyur Rinpoche.

Translated by Tyler Dewar of the Nitartha Translation Network.
© 2002 by Tyler Dewar and the Nitartha Translation Network.

# GLOSSARY

Amitabha (Tib. *'od dpag med*) The Buddha of the lotus family, lord of the pure land of Sukhavati. Amitabha is also the manifestation of the discriminating wisdom.

Anjali (Skt.) Hand mudra of divine offering.

Avalokita (Skt.) [Tib: *spyan ras gzigs/Chenrezig*] Abbreviated name of Avalokiteshvara bodhisattva of compassion.

Bardo (Skt. Antarabhava) [Tib. *bar do*] Intermediate state, usually referring to the intermediate state between death and the next rebirth. Four Bardos refer to all stages of intermediate states.

Bodhichitta (Skt. Bodhichitta) [Tib. *byang chub sems*] 'Awakened heart' A wish to end the suffering of all the beings. This term expresses the core of the Mahayana teachings of the practice of compassion and wisdom.

Dewachen (Skt. Sukhavati) [Tib. *bde ba can*] 'Blissful realm', the pure realm of Buddha Amitabha.

Dewachen prayer (Skt. Sukhavati) A prayer for all beings to take rebirth in Buddha Amitabha's pure realm of Dewachen.

Dowsing  Search for water, or minerals.

Dru bum  (Tib. *bru 'bum*) One hundred thousand syllables. A system of reciting the mantra as many hundred thousand times as there are syllables in the mantra. In this case it is 600,000 times. If the mantra contains 18 or more syllables, then only 100.000 mantras are recited.

Dzogchen  (Skt. *Mahasandhi* or *Maha ati*) [Tib. Rdzogs pa chen po/Dzogchen] Great Perfection or Ati Yoga. An advanced meditation practice that emphasises the primordial purity of the mind, and the methods for realising it. The highest teaching of the Nyingma school of Tibetan Buddhism.

Dzogpa Chenpo  see Dzogchen.

Gampopa  (Tib. *sgam po pa*).(1079-1153) Also known as dvags po lha rje, 'the Physician of Dagpo'. Main disciple of Milarepa, Gampopa was a master in the two lineages of Kadam and Mahamudra. He is seen as the founder of the Kagyu lineage. He first studied medicine and became a doctor. After the death of his wife, he became a monk and studied the Kadam tradition. He gained direct understanding of the Dharma with his master Milarepa.

Guru  (Skt.) One who is regarded as having great knowledge, wisdom and authority in a certain area, and who uses it to guide others.

King Songsten Gampo  (Tib. *srong btshan sgam p*o (569-650 or 617-650): King of Tibet who prepared the way for transmission of the Buddhist teachings. He is regarded as an incarnation of Avalokiteshvara. He married Bhrikuti of Nepal and Wen Cheng of China, who each brought a sacred statue of Buddha Shakyamuni to Lhasa. He built the first Buddhist temples in Tibet, established a code of laws based on Dharma principles and had his minister, Thönmi Sambhota, develop the Tibetan script. During his reign, the translation of Buddhist texts into Tibetan began.

Lam Rim  Progressive, graded Path.

Lakhthong  see Vipashyana.

**Lojong** (Tib. *blo sgyong*) Practice of mind training.

**Madhyamika** (Skt. Madhyamika) [Tib. *dbu ma*] The Middle Way. The highest of the four Buddhist schools of philosophy. The Middle Way means not holding any extreme views, especially those of eternalism and nihilism.

**Mahamudra** (Skt. Mahamudra) [Tib. *phyag rgya chen po*] Literally, 'The Great Seal', the ultimate view of the highest Tantras, a profound method based on direct realisation of the mind's true nature. This is the highest meditation practice within the Kagyu, Sakya, and Gelug lineages of Tibetan Buddhism.

**Mahayana** (Skt. Mahayana) [Tib. *theg pa chen po*] The vehicle of bodhisattvas striving for perfect enlightenment for the sake of all beings. One of the three great subdivisions of Buddhism, emphasizing the teachings of the Prajnaparamita on emptiness and the development of the compassionate and altruistic attitude of the bodhisattva.

**Mala** (Skt.) Rosary. The Buddhist rosary is made of 108 beads. These beads can be of various substances: wood, seeds, precious or semi-precious stones, ivory, etc.

**Mantra** (Tib. *sngags/ngak*) Literally means 'protecting the mind'. It is also a blessed and empowered sound, in form of words or syllables.

**Pandita** (Skt. Pandita) [Tib. *mkhas pa*] Learned master. Indian scholar or professor of Buddhist philosophy are usually referred to as Panditas.

**Phur ba** (Tib.) Ritual dagger.

**Pratyekabuddha** (Skt.) [Tib. *rang sangs rgyas*] 'Solitarily enlightened one', a Hinayana Arhat who attains nirvana chiefly through contemplating the 12 links of dependent origination in reverse order, without needing teachings in that lifetime. He lacks the complete realisation of Buddhahood and cannot benefit numberless sentient beings as a Buddha does.

Preliminary practices  Preliminary practices to the Mahamudra teachings, including the four common preliminaries (meditation on the 'four thoughts that turn the mind towards the Dharma', namely the precious human life, impermanence, karma and the sufferings of samsara) and the four specific preliminaries (refuge and bodhichitta, Vajrasattva purification, mandala offering and guru yoga – each being repeated 100,000 times).

Puja  (Tib) Ritual, specifically, making offerings.

Refuge Tree  We visualise a huge tree supporting on its outspread branches all the masters of the lineage, all the Buddhas, bodhisattvas, yidams, dharma protectors and representations of the dharma. This is what we call a 'refuge tree'.

Sadhana  (Skt.) [Tib. *sgrub thabs*] 'Means of accomplishment'. Tantric liturgy and procedure for practice, usually emphasizing the development stage. The typical sadhana structure involves a preliminary part, which includes the taking of refuge and arousing of bodhichitta, a main part that involves the visualization of a Buddha and the recitation of mantra, and a concluding part that involves the dissolution of the visualisation and resting one's mind in its 'natural state', the whole process being sealed by the dedication of merit to all sentient beings.

Samsara  (Skt.) [Tib. *'khor ba*] cyclic existence in which ordinary beings, trapped in an endless cycle of rebirth in the six realms, experience endless suffering.

Satori  Japanese term referring to the realisation of the nature of one's mind in the Zen tradition.

Shamatha  (Pali.) [Tib. *zhi gnas/shinay*] Calm abiding meditation.

Shravaka  (Skt. Shravaka) [Tib. *nyan thos*] 'Hearer' or 'listener'. The followers of the general and common teachings of the Buddha.

Shunyata  (Skt.) [Tib. *stong pa nyid*] The true nature or suchness of all phenomena that is devoid of true, inherent and independent existence and is beyond all levels of conceptual elaboration.

Sukhavati  (Skt) See Dewachen.

**Swastika** An ancient Indian symbol of stability and auspiciousness.

**Ten directions** The eight compass points, nadir and zenith.

**Ten bhumis** (Skt. ground or foundation) Stages or levels of attainment through which the bodhisattva passes on his/her path to enlightenment. Each serves as the basis for the next level.

**Termas** (Tib. *gter ma* 'Treasure') 1) Concealed treasures, of many different kinds including texts, ritual objects, relics and natural objects. 2) Transmission through concealed treasures, which were hidden mainly by Guru Rinpoche and Yeshe Tsogyal, to be discovered at the proper time by a terton, a 'treasure discoverer', for the benefit of future disciples.

**Three times** Past, present and future.

**Tonglen** (Tib. *gtong len*) Lit. 'taking and giving'. A bodhichitta practice of taking others' sufferings and misdeeds upon oneself and giving them one's virtue and happiness.

**Tsog** (Tib. *tshogs*) Feast offering, see below in the text for further explanations.

**Vajra** (Tib. *rdo rje / dorje*) Weapon of Indira. Something which can destroy anything but can not be destroyed by anything. A symbol of indestructible, invincible, firm and ungraspable. The ultimate vajra is emptiness.

**Vipashyana** (Skt.) [Tib. *Lhagthong*] Insight meditation, which develops insight into the nature of reality.

# ACKNOWLEDGEMENTS

We wish to thank all the people who have so kindly and patiently given their advice and help in bringing this book to fruition, celebrating the flourishing of the Dharma in Rigul, Kham, Tibet.

The Venerable Ringu Tulku Rinpoche for his precious commentary on this sadhana of Chenrezig. For Rinpoche's blessing and tireless help with overseeing the stages of this book.

All the people of Halscheid who organised the original oral teaching on the sadhana in 1998.

Corinne Segers for transcribing and editing the original teaching and Cait Collins who helped and who so kindly re-edited some of the text again in 2010.

Tyler Dewar and Snow Lion Publications for giving permission to publish this Chenrezig sadhana.

Jude Tarrant for her untiring support and guidance on helping me to see this book through to completion.

Annie Dibble for her valuable help and advice. Lama Tenam for fixing our Tibetan fonts!

Claire Trueman, Meriel Cowan, Rachel Moffitt, Dave Tuffield, Ven. Rinchen, and Jayne Whistance for their kindness in checking for mistakes in the production of this book.

R. D. Salga for his wonderful painting and drawing of Chenrezig, offered from his heart.

Francois Henrard for his amazing images taken on his visits to Rigul, Tibet.

Paul O'Connor for his inspirational and beautiful design and typesetting of the book. And for Paul's very kind and patient help.

We wish to thank the people who have generously sponsored this book.

We are pleased that 100% of all the proceeds received by Rigul Trust from the sale of this book will go to fund Rigul Trust health, education and poverty relief projects. This will help to bring benefit to all the children, the teachers, the cooks, the health clinic, the doctor, his assistant, the nurse, and all the people in Rigul, Tibet.

And finally we dedicate this book to the people of Rigul, Tibet, for all who find inspiration and joy in their hearts from Ringu Tulku Rinpoche's commentary on this Chenrezig sadhana and for the benefit of all beings everywhere.

May all beings be SAFE. May all beings be HAPPY. May all beings be PEACEFUL. May all beings be FREE.  May all beings AWAKEN to the light of their TRUE NATURE.

Margaret Richardson
*Rigul Trust*

ༀ་མ་ཎི་པདྨེ་ཧཱུྃ

# COMMEMORATING RINGU TULKU RINPOCHE'S HOMELAND IN TIBET

This is a commemorative book to celebrate the flourishing of the Dharma, the monastery, the health clinic and the school in Rigul, Kham, Tibet, the birthplace of Ringu Tulku Rinpoche.

Through many bleak years, the continuation of the practice of Buddhadharma in Rigul has been made especially possible by the devotional and dedicated efforts of all the khenpos, the tulkus and the lamas of Rigul monastery. Ringu Tulku Rinpoche is the abbot of the monastery, having to operate from a position of exile and lives in Sikkim, India.

All the people of Rigul and the surrounding area have spent years experiencing extreme poverty and hard labour. From the depths of their being they have summoned up the strength and the courage, the resolve and the determination, to maintain the spirit and welfare of their community by helping each other in very trying times for the last fifty years.

So much has been, and is being, achieved in very difficult and challenging circumstances. The monastery has been reconstructed and in August 2009 thousands of people came to Rigul monastery for teachings and blessings to mark the great occasion of the opening of the shedra. This big inauguration was presided over by Dulmo Choje Rinpoche, as the chief guest, with over eight hundred monks and nuns attending the opening ceremony including high Rinpoches, khenpos and lamas.

In recent years a purpose built health clinic and school have been built, which serve the wider community.

The monastery, the health clinic and the school have been supported, financially, in prayer, in kind and in deed, by students, friends and family of Ringu Tulku from every walk of life, from all over the world.

All of this is fulfilling one of Ringu Tulku's dreams. A celebration of the wisdom and compassion that shines through Ringu Tulku Rinpoche's inspiration and initiative in developing the monastery, of which he is the abbot, the health clinic and the school from afar in geographical terms but steadfastly held within his heart.

Margaret Richardson
*Founder, Rigul Trust*

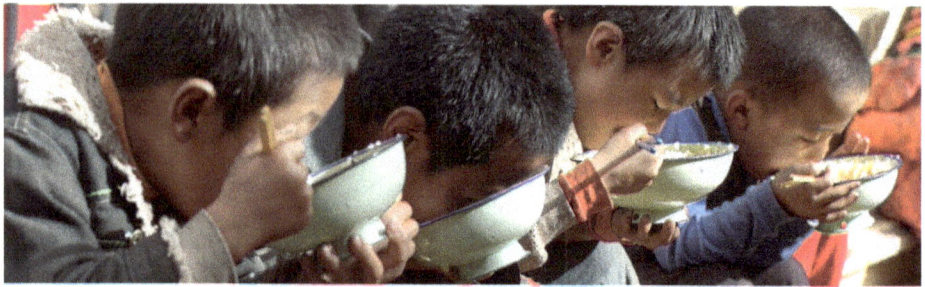

Rigul Trust is a UK Charity whose main aim is to provide funds for the provision of basic health care, education and poverty relief amongst Tibetan refugee communities in India, and in particular for the people of some of the most remote areas of Tibet, such as Rigul.

In Rigul, we currently fund:
The school, including free school meals and the teachers' and cooks' salaries.
The health clinic, funding the doctor, the nurse and the running costs of the clinic.
The shedra, funding the Khenpo and food for the monks.

TO FIND OUT MORE, OR TO MAKE A DONATION, PLEASE VISIT:
# www.rigultrust.org
info@rigultrust.org & donations@rigultrust

Patron: Ringu Tulku Rinpoche  -  Founder: Margaret Richardson  -  UK Charity Registration No: 1124076

www.ingramcontent.com/pod-product-compliance
Lightning Source LLC
Chambersburg PA
CBHW061153010526
44118CB00027B/2961